Life is
sweet

Life is sweet

Over 100 tempting sweet recipes

First published in 2012
LOVE FOOD is an imprint of Parragon Books Ltd

Parragon
Chartist House
15–17 Trim Street
Bath, BA1 1HA, UK

www.parragon.com/lovefood

ISBN: 978-1-78186-838-6

Printed in China

Internal design by Pink Creative

Notes for the Reader
This book uses both metric and imperial measurements. Follow the same units of measurement throughout; do not mix metric and imperial. All spoon measurements are level: teaspoons are assumed to be 5 ml, and tablespoons are assumed to be 15 ml. Unless otherwise stated, milk is assumed to be full fat, eggs and individual vegetables are medium, and pepper is freshly ground black pepper. Unless otherwise stated, all root vegetables should be washed in plain water and peeled prior to using.

Garnishes, decorations and serving suggestions are all optional and not necessarily included in the recipe ingredients or method.

The times given are an approximate guide only. Preparation times differ according to the techniques used by different people and the cooking times may also vary from those given. Optional ingredients, variations or serving suggestions have not been included in the time calculations.

Recipes using raw or very lightly cooked eggs should be avoided by infants, the elderly, pregnant women, convalescents and anyone suffering from an illness. Pregnant and breastfeeding women are advised to avoid eating peanuts and peanut products. Sufferers from nut allergies should be aware that some of the ready-made ingredients used in the recipes in this book may contain nuts. Always check the packaging before use.

Vegetarians should be aware that some of the ready-made ingredients used in the recipes in this book may contain animal products. Always check the packaging before use.

CONTENTS

INTRODUCTION

If you have a seriously sweet tooth and cannot get by without a daily chocolate fix or contemplate an afternoon cuppa without its cookie accompaniment, this is the perfect cookbook for you!

This fantastic collection contains over 100 recipes for all manner of sweet temptations. Flick through the pages to find irresistible recipes for every occasion – whether you fancy a 'little something' between meals, like a dainty cupcake, or are looking for an indulgent dessert to round off a meal. From comforting fruit pies to brighten up a winter's day to enticing ice creams and sorbets to cool you down when the heat is on, there are dishes for all moods and seasons. In fact, there is so much variety that you are guaranteed to find a recipe to satisfy those sugar cravings, whenever they strike!

YUMMY

Recipes for the chocoholic

CHOCOLATE FUDGE CAKE

Preheat the oven to 180°C/350°F/Gas Mark 4. Grease and line the bases of 2 x 20-cm/8-inch sandwich tins.

To make the icing, place the chocolate, muscovado sugar, butter, evaporated milk and vanilla extract in a heavy-based saucepan. Heat gently, stirring constantly, until melted. Pour into a bowl and leave to cool. Cover and chill in the refrigerator for 1 hour, or until spreadable.

For the cake, place the butter and caster sugar in a bowl and beat together until light and fluffy. Gradually beat in the eggs. Stir in the golden syrup and ground almonds. Sift the flour, salt and cocoa powder into a separate bowl, then fold into the mixture. Add a little water, if necessary, to make a dropping consistency.

Spoon the mixture into the prepared tins and bake in the preheated oven for 30–35 minutes, or until springy to the touch and a skewer inserted in the centre comes out clean.

Leave the cakes in the tins for 5 minutes, then turn out onto wire racks to cool completely. When the cakes are cold, sandwich them together with half the icing. Spread the remaining icing over the top and sides of the cake, swirling it to give a frosted appearance.

Serves 8

175 g/6 oz unsalted butter, softened, plus extra for greasing

175 g/6 oz golden caster sugar

3 eggs, beaten

3 tbsp golden syrup

40 g/1½ oz ground almonds

175 g/6 oz self-raising flour

pinch of salt

40 g/1½ oz cocoa powder

Icing

225 g/8 oz plain chocolate, broken into pieces

55 g/2 oz dark muscovado sugar

225 g/8 oz unsalted butter, diced

5 tbsp evaporated milk

½ tsp vanilla extract

BLACK FOREST GATEAU

Serves 8

900 g/2 lb fresh cherries, stoned and halved

250 g/9 oz caster sugar

100 ml/3½ fl oz cherry brandy

100 g/3½ oz plain flour

50 g/1¾ oz cocoa powder

½ tsp baking powder

4 eggs

3 tbsp unsalted butter, melted, plus extra for greasing

1 litre/1¾ pints double cream

To decorate

grated plain chocolate

whole fresh cherries

Preheat the oven to 180°C/350°F/Gas Mark 4. Grease and line a 23-cm/9-inch round springform cake tin.

Place the cherries in a saucepan, add 3 tablespoons of the sugar and the cherry brandy and bring to a simmer over a medium heat. Simmer for 5 minutes. Drain, reserving the syrup.

In a large bowl, sift together the flour, cocoa powder and baking powder. Place the eggs in a heatproof bowl and beat in 160 g/5¾ oz of the remaining sugar. Place the bowl over a saucepan of simmering water and beat for 6 minutes, or until thickened. Remove from the heat, then gradually fold in the flour mixture and melted butter. Spoon into the prepared cake tin and bake in the preheated oven for 40 minutes. Remove from the oven and leave to cool in the tin.

Turn out the cake and cut in half horizontally. Mix the double cream and the remaining sugar together and whip lightly until soft peaks form. Spread the reserved syrup over the cut sides of the cake, then spread a layer of whipped cream on the bottom half of the cake, followed by the cherries, and then place the other half on top. Cover the top of the cake with whipped cream, sprinkle over the grated chocolate and decorate with whole fresh cherries.

DOUBLE CHOCOLATE BROWNIES

Preheat the oven to 180°C/350°F/Gas Mark 4. Grease an 18-cm/7-inch square cake tin and line the base with baking paper.

Place the butter and chocolate in a small heatproof bowl set over a saucepan of gently simmering water until melted. Stir until smooth. Leave to cool slightly. Stir in the sugar, salt and vanilla extract. Add the eggs, one at a time, and stir until blended.

Sift the flour and cocoa powder into the mixture and beat until smooth. Stir in the chocolate chips, then pour the mixture into the prepared tin. Bake in the preheated oven for 35–40 minutes, or until the top is evenly coloured and a skewer inserted into the centre comes out almost clean. Leave to cool slightly while you prepare the sauce.

To make the fudge sauce, place the butter, sugar, milk, cream and golden syrup in a small saucepan and heat gently until the sugar has dissolved. Bring to the boil and stir for 10 minutes, or until the mixture is caramel-coloured. Remove from the heat and add the chocolate. Stir until smooth. Cut the brownies into squares and serve immediately with the sauce.

Makes 9

115 g/4 oz butter, plus extra for greasing

115 g/4 oz plain chocolate, broken into pieces

300 g/10½ oz golden caster sugar

pinch of salt

1 tsp vanilla extract

2 large eggs

140 g/5 oz plain flour

2 tbsp cocoa powder

100 g/3½ oz white chocolate chips

Fudge sauce

4 tbsp butter

225 g/8 oz golden caster sugar

150 ml/5 fl oz milk

250 ml/9 fl oz double cream

225 g/8 oz golden syrup

200 g/7 oz plain chocolate, broken into pieces

CHEESECAKE BROWNIES

Makes 12

175 g/6 oz butter, plus extra for greasing

3 tbsp cocoa powder

200 g/7 oz caster sugar

2 eggs, beaten

125 g/4½ oz plain flour

Cheesecake mix

250 g/9 oz ricotta cheese

40 g/1½ oz golden caster sugar

1 egg, beaten

Preheat the oven to 180°C/350°F/Gas Mark 4. Grease a 28 x 18-cm/11 x 7-inch rectangular baking tin.

Melt the butter in a medium saucepan, remove from the heat and stir in the cocoa powder and sugar. Beat in the eggs, then add the flour and stir to mix evenly. Pour into the prepared tin.

For the cheesecake mix, beat together the ricotta, sugar and egg, then drop teaspoonfuls of the mixture over the chocolate mixture. Use a palette knife to swirl the two mixtures together lightly.

Bake in the preheated oven for 40–45 minutes, until just firm to the touch. Cool in the tin, then cut into rectangles or squares.

DOUBLE CHOCOLATE MUFFINS

Preheat the oven to 190°C/375°F/Gas Mark 5. Place 12 paper muffin cases in a muffin tin.

Put the butter, caster sugar and muscovado sugar into a bowl and beat well. Beat in the eggs, soured cream and milk until thoroughly mixed. Sift the flour, bicarbonate of soda and cocoa powder into a separate bowl and stir into the mixture. Add the chocolate chips and mix well.

Spoon the mixture into the paper cases. Bake in the preheated oven for 25–30 minutes. Remove from the oven and leave to cool for 10 minutes. Turn out onto a wire rack and leave to cool completely.

Makes 12

100 g/3½ oz butter, softened

125 g/4½ oz caster sugar

100 g/3½ oz dark muscovado sugar

2 eggs

150 ml/5 fl oz soured cream

5 tbsp milk

250 g/9 oz plain flour

1 tsp bicarbonate of soda

2 tbsp cocoa powder

190 g/6½ oz plain chocolate chips

CHOCOLATE BUTTERFLY CAKES

Makes 12

125 g/4½ oz soft margarine

125 g/4½ oz caster sugar

150 g/5½ oz self-raising flour

2 large eggs

2 tbsp cocoa powder

25 g/1 oz plain chocolate, melted

icing sugar, for dusting

Lemon buttercream

100 g/3½ oz unsalted butter, softened

225 g/8 oz icing sugar, sifted

grated rind of ½ lemon

1 tbsp lemon juice

Preheat the oven to 180°C/350°F/Gas Mark 4. Place 12 paper bun cases in a shallow bun tin.

Place the margarine, caster sugar, flour, eggs and cocoa powder in a large bowl and beat with an electric whisk until the mixture is just smooth. Beat in the melted chocolate.

Spoon the mixture into the paper cases, filling them three quarters full. Bake in the preheated oven for 15 minutes, or until springy to the touch. Transfer to a wire rack and leave to cool completely.

Meanwhile, make the lemon buttercream. Place the butter in a mixing bowl and beat until fluffy, then gradually beat in the icing sugar. Beat in the lemon rind and gradually add the lemon juice, beating well.

Cut the top off each cake, using a serrated knife. Cut each cake top in half. Spread or pipe the lemon buttercream over the cut surface of each cake and push the two cut pieces of cake top into the icing to form wings. Dust with icing sugar.

DEVIL'S FOOD CAKES WITH CHOCOLATE ICING

Preheat the oven to 180°C/350°F/Gas Mark 4. Put 18 paper bun cases in a bun tin, or put 18 double-layer paper cases on a baking tray.

Put the margarine, sugar, eggs, flour, bicarbonate of soda and cocoa powder in a large bowl and, using an electric hand whisk, beat together until just smooth. Using a metal spoon, fold in the soured cream. Spoon the mixture into the paper cases.

Bake the cupcakes in the preheated oven for 20 minutes, or until well risen and firm to the touch. Transfer to a wire rack to cool.

To make the icing, break the chocolate into a heatproof bowl. Set the bowl over a saucepan of gently simmering water and heat until melted, stirring occasionally. Remove from the heat and allow to cool slightly, then whisk in the sugar and soured cream until combined. Spread the icing over the tops of the cupcakes and leave to set in the refrigerator before serving. Serve decorated with chocolate caraque.

Makes 18

50 g/1¾ oz soft tub margarine
115 g/4 oz soft dark brown sugar
2 large eggs
115 g/4 oz plain flour
½ tsp bicarbonate of soda
25 g/1 oz cocoa powder
125 ml/4 fl oz soured cream
chocolate caraque, to decorate

Icing

125 g/4½ oz plain chocolate
2 tbsp caster sugar
150 ml/5 fl oz soured cream

DOUBLE CHOC COOKIES

Makes about 30

225 g/8 oz butter, softened

140 g/5 oz caster sugar

1 egg yolk, lightly beaten

2 tsp vanilla extract

250 g/9 oz plain flour

25 g/1 oz cocoa powder

pinch of salt

350 g/12 oz plain chocolate, chopped

55 g/2 oz dried sour cherries

Preheat the oven to 190°C/375°F/Gas Mark 5. Line 2 baking trays with baking paper.

Put the butter and sugar into a bowl and mix well with a wooden spoon, then beat in the egg yolk and vanilla extract. Sift together the flour, cocoa and salt into the mixture, add the chopped chocolate and sour cherries and stir until thoroughly combined.

Scoop up tablespoons of the mixture and shape into balls. Put them on the prepared baking trays, spaced well apart, and flatten slightly.

Bake in the preheated oven for 12–15 minutes. Leave to cool on the baking trays for 5–10 minutes, then carefully transfer to wire racks to cool completely.

CHOCOLATE CARAMEL SHORTBREAD

Preheat the oven to 180°C/350°F/Gas Mark 4. Grease and line the base of a 23-cm/9-inch square shallow cake tin.

Place the butter, flour and sugar in a food processor and process until it begins to bind together. Press the mixture into the prepared tin and smooth the top. Bake in the preheated oven for 20–25 minutes, or until golden.

Meanwhile, make the filling. Place the butter, sugar, golden syrup and condensed milk in a saucepan and heat gently until the sugar has dissolved. Bring to the boil and simmer for 6–8 minutes, stirring constantly, until the mixture becomes very thick. Pour over the shortbread base and leave to chill in the refrigerator until firm.

To make the topping, place the chocolate in a heatproof bowl set over a saucepan of gently simmering water and stir until melted. Leave to cool slightly, then spread over the caramel. Chill in the refrigerator until set. Cut the shortbread into 12 pieces with a sharp knife and serve.

Makes 12

115 g/4 oz butter, plus extra for greasing

175 g/6 oz plain flour

55 g/2 oz golden caster sugar

Filling & topping

175 g/6 oz butter

115 g/4 oz golden caster sugar

3 tbsp golden syrup

400 g/14 oz canned condensed milk

200 g/7 oz plain chocolate, broken into pieces

NO-BAKE CHOCOLATE CAKE

Serves 6–8

225 g/8 oz plain chocolate

225 g/8 oz unsalted butter, plus extra for greasing

3 tbsp black coffee

55 g/2 oz soft light brown sugar

a few drops of vanilla extract

225 g/8 oz digestive biscuits, crushed

85 g/3 oz raisins

85 g/3 oz walnuts, chopped

Grease and line a 450-g/1-lb loaf tin.

Place the chocolate, butter, coffee, sugar and vanilla extract in a saucepan over a low heat and stir until the chocolate and butter have melted, the sugar has dissolved and the mixture is well combined.

Stir in the crushed biscuits, the raisins and walnuts and stir well.

Spoon the mixture into the prepared loaf tin. Leave to set for 1–2 hours in the refrigerator, then turn out and cut into thin slices to serve.

CHOCOLATE &
VANILLA MARBLED LOAF

Preheat the oven to 160°C/325°F/Gas Mark 3. Grease a 450-g/1-lb loaf tin and line the base with baking paper. Dust a little flour around the inside of the tin, shaking out the excess.

Break up the chocolate, place in a small heatproof bowl with the milk and set over a saucepan of simmering water. Heat gently until just melted. Remove from the heat.

Cream together the butter and sugar until light and fluffy. Beat in the egg and soured cream. Sift the flour and baking powder into the mixture, then fold in lightly and evenly using a metal spoon.

Spoon half the mixture into a separate bowl and stir in the chocolate mixture. Add the vanilla extract to the plain mixture.

Spoon the chocolate and vanilla mixtures alternately into the prepared loaf tin, swirling lightly with a knife or skewer for a marbled effect. Bake in the preheated oven for 40–45 minutes, or until well-risen and firm to the touch.

Cool in the tin for 10 minutes, then turn out and finish cooling on a wire rack.

Serves 8

55 g/2 oz plain chocolate

3 tbsp milk

70 g/2½ oz unsalted butter, plus extra for greasing

85 g/3 oz caster sugar

1 egg, beaten

3 tbsp soured cream

115 g/4 oz self-raising flour, plus extra for dusting

½ tsp baking powder

½ tsp vanilla extract

CHOCOLATE BROWNIE ROULADE

Serves 6

butter, for greasing

150 g/5½ oz plain chocolate, broken into pieces

3 tbsp water

175 g/6 oz caster sugar

5 eggs, separated

25 g/1 oz raisins, chopped

25 g/1 oz pecan nuts, chopped

pinch of salt

icing sugar, for dusting

300 ml/10 fl oz double cream, lightly whipped

Preheat the oven to 180°C/350°F/Gas Mark 4. Grease a 30 x 20-cm/12 x 8-inch Swiss roll tin and line with baking paper.

Melt the chocolate with the water in a small saucepan over a low heat until the chocolate has melted. Leave to cool.

In a bowl, whisk the sugar and egg yolks for 2–3 minutes with an electric hand-held whisk until thick and pale. Fold in the cooled chocolate, the raisins and pecan nuts.

In a separate bowl, whisk the egg whites with the salt. Fold one quarter of the egg whites into the chocolate mixture, then fold in the rest of the whites, working lightly and quickly.

Transfer the mixture to the prepared tin and bake in the preheated oven for 25 minutes, until risen and just firm to the touch. Leave to cool before covering with a sheet of baking paper and a damp clean tea towel. Leave until cold.

Turn the roulade out onto another piece of baking paper dusted with icing sugar and carefully remove the lining paper.

Spread the cream over the roulade. Starting from a short end, roll the sponge away from you using the paper to guide you. Trim the ends of the roulade to make a neat finish and transfer to a serving plate. Leave to chill in the refrigerator. Dust with icing sugar before serving.

INDIVIDUAL CHOCOLATE PUDDINGS

Grease 4 x 175-ml/6-fl oz pudding basins.

To make the puddings, put the sugar and eggs into a heatproof bowl and place over a saucepan of simmering water. Whisk for about 10 minutes, until frothy. Remove the bowl from the heat and fold in the flour and cocoa powder. Fold in the butter, then the chocolate. Mix well.

Spoon the mixture into the prepared pudding basins and cover with baking paper. Top with foil and secure with string. Place the puddings in a large saucepan filled with enough simmering water to reach halfway up the sides of the basins. Steam for about 40 minutes, or until cooked through.

About 2–3 minutes before the end of the cooking time, make the sauce. Put the butter, chocolate, water and sugar into a small saucepan and warm over a low heat, stirring constantly, until melted and combined. Stir in the liqueur.

Remove the puddings from the heat, turn out onto serving dishes and pour over the sauce. Decorate with coffee beans and serve.

Serves 4

Puddings
100 g/3½ oz caster sugar

3 eggs

75 g/2¾ oz plain flour, sifted

50 g/1¾ oz cocoa powder, sifted

100 g/3½ oz unsalted butter, melted, plus extra for greasing

100 g/3½ oz plain chocolate, melted

Chocolate sauce
2 tbsp unsalted butter

100 g/3½ oz plain chocolate

5 tbsp water

1 tbsp caster sugar

1 tbsp coffee liqueur

coffee beans, to decorate

CHOCOLATE CRUMBLE PIE

Serves 8

Pastry

175 g/6 oz plain flour

1 tsp baking powder

115 g/4 oz unsalted butter, cut into small pieces

55 g/2 oz caster sugar

1 egg yolk

1–2 tsp cold water

Filling

150 ml/5 fl oz double cream

150 ml/5 fl oz milk

225 g/8 oz plain chocolate, chopped

2 eggs

Crumble topping

85 g/3 oz toasted pecan nuts

115 g/4 oz plain chocolate

85 g/3 oz amaretti biscuits

115 g/4 oz soft light brown sugar

1 tsp cocoa powder

To make the pastry, sift the flour and baking powder into a large bowl. Rub in the butter and stir in the sugar, then add the egg and the water to bring the dough together. Turn the dough out and knead briefly. Wrap and chill in the refrigerator for 30 minutes.

Preheat the oven to 190°C/375°F/Gas Mark 5.

Roll out the pastry and use it to line a 23-cm/9-inch round loose-based flan tin. Prick the base with a fork. Line with baking paper, fill with baking beans and bake in the preheated oven for 15 minutes. Remove the paper and beans. Reduce the oven temperature to 180°C/350°F/Gas Mark 4.

To make the filling, bring the cream and milk to the boil in a saucepan, remove from the heat and add the chocolate. Stir until melted and smooth. Beat the eggs and add to the chocolate mixture, mix well and pour into the pastry case. Bake for 15 minutes, remove from the oven and leave to rest for 1 hour.

When you are ready to serve the pie, chop the pecan nuts and chocolate with a large knife and crush the biscuits. Place in a large bowl, then add the sugar and cocoa and mix well. Sprinkle over the pie, then cut into slices and serve.

MISSISSIPPI MUD PIE

Preheat the oven to 180°C/350°F/Gas Mark 4. Lightly grease a 23-cm/9-inch round springform or loose-based cake tin.

To make the crumb crust, put the digestive biscuits, pecan nuts, sugar and cinnamon into a food processor and process until fine crumbs form – do not overprocess to a powder. Add the melted butter and process again until moistened.

Tip the crumb mixture into the prepared cake tin and press over the base and about 4 cm/1½ inches up the sides of the tin. Cover the tin and chill while you make the filling.

To make the filling, put the butter, chocolate and golden syrup into a saucepan over a low heat and stir until melted and blended. Leave to cool, then beat in the eggs and pecan nuts.

Pour the filling into the chilled crumb crust and smooth the surface. Bake in the preheated oven for 30 minutes, or until just set but still soft in the centre. Leave to cool on a wire rack. Serve at room temperature or chilled.

Serves 12–14

Crumb crust

140 g/5 oz digestive biscuits

85 g/3 oz pecan nuts, finely chopped

1 tbsp soft light brown sugar

½ tsp ground cinnamon

85 g/3 oz butter, melted, plus extra for greasing

Filling

225 g/8 oz butter or margarine

175 g/6 oz plain chocolate, chopped

125 ml/4 fl oz golden syrup

4 large eggs, beaten

85 g/3 oz pecan nuts, finely chopped

DEEP CHOCOLATE CHEESECAKE

Serves 6–8

Base

115 g/4 oz digestive biscuits, finely crushed

2 tsp cocoa powder

55 g/2 oz butter, melted, plus extra for greasing

Chocolate layer

800 g/1 lb 12 oz mascarpone cheese

200 g/7 oz icing sugar, sifted

juice of ½ orange

finely grated rind of 1 orange

175 g/6 oz plain chocolate

2 tbsp brandy

chocolate leaves, to decorate

Grease a 20-cm/8-inch round loose-based cake tin.

To make the base, put the crushed biscuits, cocoa powder and melted butter into a large bowl and mix well. Press the biscuit mixture evenly over the base of the prepared tin.

Put the mascarpone cheese and icing sugar into a bowl and stir in the orange juice and rind. Place the chocolate in a heatproof bowl set over a saucepan of gently simmering water until melted. Leave to cool slightly, then stir in the brandy. Add to the mascarpone cheese mixture and mix together until thoroughly combined. Spread the chocolate mixture evenly over the biscuit layer. Cover with clingfilm and chill for at least 4 hours.

Remove the cheesecake from the refrigerator, turn out onto a serving platter and decorate with chocolate leaves. Serve immediately.

PROFITEROLES

Preheat the oven to 200°C/400°F/Gas Mark 6. Grease a large baking tray.

To make the pastry, place the butter and water in a saucepan and bring to the boil. Meanwhile, sift the flour into a bowl. Turn off the heat and beat in the flour until smooth. Cool for 5 minutes. Beat in enough of the eggs to give the mixture a soft, dropping consistency.

Transfer to a piping bag fitted with a 1-cm/½-inch plain nozzle. Pipe small balls onto the prepared baking tray. Bake in the preheated oven for 25 minutes.

Remove from the oven. Pierce each ball with a skewer to let the steam escape.

To make the filling, whip the cream, sugar and vanilla extract together. Cut the pastry balls across the middle, then fill with cream.

To make the sauce, gently melt the chocolate, butter and water together in a small saucepan, stirring constantly, until smooth. Stir in the brandy.

Pile the profiteroles into individual serving dishes, pour over the sauce and serve.

Serves 4

Choux pastry
70 g/2½ oz unsalted butter, plus extra for greasing
200 ml/7 fl oz water
100 g/3½ oz plain flour
3 eggs, beaten

Cream filling
300 ml/10 fl oz double cream
3 tbsp caster sugar
1 tsp vanilla extract

Chocolate & brandy sauce
125 g/4½ oz plain chocolate, broken into small pieces
35 g/1¼ oz unsalted butter
6 tbsp water
2 tbsp brandy

CHOCOLATE MOUSSE

Serves 4–6

225 g/8 oz plain chocolate, chopped

2 tbsp brandy, Grand Marnier or Cointreau

4 tbsp water

30 g/1 oz unsalted butter, diced

3 large eggs, separated

¼ tsp cream of tartar

55 g/2 oz caster sugar

125 ml/4 fl oz double cream

Place the chocolate, brandy and water in a small saucepan over a low heat and melt, stirring, until smooth. Remove the saucepan from the heat and beat in the butter.

Beat the egg yolks into the chocolate mixture, one after another, until blended, then leave to cool slightly.

Meanwhile, using an electric hand-held whisk on low speed, beat the egg whites in a spotlessly clean bowl until they are frothy, then gradually increase the mixer's speed and beat until soft peaks form. Sprinkle the cream of tartar over the surface, then add the sugar, tablespoon by tablespoon, and continue beating until stiff peaks form. Beat several tablespoons of the egg whites into the chocolate mixture to loosen.

In another bowl, whip the cream until soft peaks form. Spoon the cream over the chocolate mixture, then spoon the remaining whites over the cream. Use a large metal spoon or rubber spatula to fold the chocolate into the cream and egg whites.

Divide the chocolate mousse between 4–6 individual serving bowls. Cover with clingfilm and chill the mousse for at least 3 hours before serving.

CHOCOLATE ICE-CREAM BITES

Line a baking tray with clingfilm.

Using a melon baller, scoop out balls of ice cream and place them on the prepared baking tray. Alternatively, cut the ice cream into bite-sized cubes. Stick a cocktail stick in each piece and return to the freezer until very hard.

Place the chocolate and the butter in a heatproof bowl set over a saucepan of gently simmering water until melted. Quickly dip the frozen ice-cream balls into the warm chocolate and return to the freezer. Keep them there until ready to serve.

Serves 6

600 ml/1 pint good-quality ice cream

200 g/7 oz plain chocolate

2 tbsp unsalted butter

CHOCOLATE ICE CREAM

Serves 4–6

300 ml/10 fl oz milk
1 vanilla pod
100 g/3½ oz plain chocolate
3 egg yolks
85 g/3 oz castor sugar
300 ml/10 fl oz double cream

Pour the milk into a large heavy-based saucepan, split open the vanilla pod and scrape out the seeds into the milk and add the whole vanilla pod. Bring almost to the boil then remove from the heat and leave to infuse for 30 minutes. Remove the vanilla pod from the milk. Break the chocolate into the milk and heat gently, stirring all the time, until melted and smooth.

Put the egg yolks and sugar in a large bowl and whisk together until pale and the mixture leaves a trail when the whisk is lifted. Slowly add the chocolate mixture, stirring all the time with a wooden spoon. Strain the mixture into the rinsed-out saucepan or a double boiler and cook over a low heat for 10–15 minutes, stirring all the time, until the mixture thickens enough to coat the back of a wooden spoon. Do not allow the mixture to boil or it will curdle. Remove the custard from the heat and leave to cool for at least 1 hour, stirring from time to time to prevent a skin from forming. Meanwhile, whip the cream until it holds its shape. Keep in the refrigerator until ready to use.

If using an ice cream machine, fold the whipped cream into the cold custard, then churn the mixture in the machine following the manufacturer's instructions. Alternatively, freeze the custard in a freezerproof container, uncovered, for 1–2 hours, or until it begins to set around the edges. Turn the custard into a bowl and stir with a fork or beat in a food processor until smooth. Fold in the whipped cream. Return to the freezer and freeze for a further 2–3 hours, or until firm. Cover the container with a lid for storing.

CHOCOLATE CREAMS

Line a baking tray with baking paper.

Melt 55 g/2 oz of the chocolate in a large heatproof bowl set over a saucepan of gently simmering water. Stir in the cream and remove the bowl from the heat.

Sift the icing sugar into the melted chocolate, then mix together well. Knead to form a firm, smooth, pliable mixture.

Lightly dust a work surface with cocoa powder, turn out the mixture and roll out to a 5-mm/¼-inch thickness. Stamp out rounds, using a 2.5-cm/ 1-inch plain round cutter.

Transfer to the prepared baking tray and leave to stand for about 12 hours or overnight, until set and dry.

When the chocolate creams have set, line a baking tray with baking paper. Melt the remaining chocolate in a heatproof bowl set over a saucepan of gently simmering water. Using 2 forks, carefully dip each chocolate cream into the melted chocolate. Lift it out quickly, letting any excess chocolate drip back into the bowl, and place on the prepared baking tray. Leave to set.

Makes about 30

200 g/7 oz plain chocolate, broken into pieces

2 tbsp single cream

225 g/8 oz icing sugar

cocoa powder, for dusting

WHITE CHOCOLATE TRUFFLES

Makes 20

25 g/1 oz unsalted butter

5 tbsp double cream

325 g/11½ oz white chocolate, broken into pieces

1 tbsp orange liqueur (optional)

Line a Swiss roll tin with baking paper.

Place the butter and cream in a small saucepan and bring slowly to the boil, stirring constantly. Boil for 1 minute, then remove from the heat.

Add 225 g/8 oz of the chocolate to the cream. Stir until melted, then beat in the liqueur, if using. Pour into the prepared tin and chill for about 2 hours, until firm.

Break off pieces of the mixture and roll them into balls. Chill for a further 30 minutes before finishing the truffles.

To finish, put the remaining chocolate in a heatproof bowl set over a saucepan of gently simmering water until melted. Dip the balls in the chocolate, letting any excess chocolate drip back into the bowl. Place on baking paper, swirl the chocolate with the tines of a fork and let it harden.

ITALIAN CHOCOLATE TRUFFLES

Melt the chocolate with the amaretto in a heatproof bowl set over a saucepan of gently simmering water, stirring until well combined.

Add the butter and stir until it has melted. Stir in the icing sugar and the ground almonds.

Leave the mixture in a cool place until firm enough to roll into 24 balls.

Place the grated chocolate on a plate and roll the truffles in the chocolate to coat them.

Place the truffles in paper sweet cases and chill.

Makes 24

175 g/6 oz plain chocolate, broken into pieces

2 tbsp amaretto or orange liqueur

3 tbsp unsalted butter

4 tbsp icing sugar

50 g/1¾ oz ground almonds

50 g/1¾ oz grated chocolate

ROCKY ROAD BITES

Makes 18

125 g/4½ oz milk chocolate, broken into pieces

40 g/1½ oz mini marshmallows

25 g/1 oz chopped walnuts

25 g/1 oz ready-to-eat dried apricots, chopped

Line a baking tray with baking paper and set aside.

Put the chocolate in a large heatproof bowl set over a saucepan of gently simmering water and stir until the chocolate has melted.

Stir in the marshmallows, walnuts and apricots, and toss in the melted chocolate until well covered.

Put heaped teaspoonfuls of the mixture on the prepared baking tray.

Let the sweets chill in the refrigerator until set. Once set, carefully remove the sweets from the baking paper.

CHOCOLATE FONDUE

Using a sharp knife, peel and core the pineapple, then cut the flesh into cubes. Peel the mango, remove the stone and cut the flesh into cubes. Peel back the papery outer skin of the physalis and twist at the top to make a 'handle'. Arrange all the fruit on 6 serving plates and leave to chill in the refrigerator.

To make the fondue, place the chocolate and cream in a fondue pot. Heat gently, stirring constantly, until the chocolate has melted. Stir in the brandy until thoroughly blended and the chocolate mixture is smooth.

Place the fondue pot over the burner to keep warm. To serve, allow each guest to dip the fruit into the sauce using fondue forks or bamboo skewers.

Serves 6

1 pineapple

1 mango

12 physalis

250 g/9 oz fresh strawberries

250 g/9 oz seedless green grapes

Fondue

250 g/9 oz plain chocolate, broken into pieces

150 ml/5 fl oz double cream

2 tbsp brandy

HOT CHOCOLATE FLOAT

Serves 4

450 ml/16 fl oz milk

225 g/8 oz plain chocolate

2 tbsp caster sugar

8 scoops coconut ice cream

8 scoops plain chocolate ice cream

whipped cream, to decorate

Pour the milk into a saucepan. Break the chocolate into small pieces and add to the saucepan with the sugar. Stir over a low heat until the chocolate has melted, the sugar has dissolved and the mixture is smooth. Remove the saucepan from the heat.

Put 1 scoop of coconut ice cream into each of 4 tall heatproof glasses, top with a scoop of chocolate ice cream, then repeat the layers.

Pour the chocolate-flavoured milk into the glasses, top with whipped cream and serve immediately.

SCRUMMY

Cakes for all occasions

ICED FAIRY CAKES

Preheat the oven to 190°C/375°F/Gas Mark 5.
Place 16 paper bun cases in a shallow bun tin.

Place the butter and caster sugar in a large bowl
and cream together with a wooden spoon or
electric mixer until pale and fluffy.

Gradually add the eggs, beating well after each
addition. Fold in the flour lightly and evenly using
a metal spoon.

Divide the mixture evenly between the paper
cases and bake in the preheated oven for
15–20 minutes. Cool on a wire rack.

For the icing, sift the icing sugar into a bowl and
stir in just enough of the water to mix to a smooth
paste that is thick enough to coat the back
of a wooden spoon. Stir in a few drops of food
colouring, if using. Spread the icing over the fairy
cakes and decorate as desired.

Makes 16

115 g/4 oz unsalted butter,
softened

115 g/4 oz caster sugar

2 eggs, beaten

115 g/4 oz self-raising flour

Icing & decoration

200 g/7 oz icing sugar

about 2 tbsp warm water

a few drops of edible food
colouring (optional)

sugar flowers, hundreds and
thousands, glacé cherries,
and/or chocolate strands,
to decorate

RASPBERRY ALMOND CUPCAKES

Makes 14

115 g/4 oz butter, softened
85 g/3 oz caster sugar
½ tsp almond extract
2 eggs, lightly beaten
85 g/3 oz self raising flour
55 g/2 oz ground almonds
85 g/3 oz fresh raspberries
2 tbsp flaked almonds
icing sugar, for dusting

Preheat the oven to 180°C/350°F/Gas Mark 4. Put 14 paper bun cases in 2 bun tins or put 14 double-layer paper cases on a baking tray.

Put the butter, sugar and almond extract in a bowl and beat together until light and fluffy. Gradually beat in the eggs. Sift in the flour and, using a metal spoon, fold into the mixture with the ground almonds. Gently fold in the raspberries. Spoon the mixture into the paper cases. Scatter the flaked almonds over the top.

Bake the cupcakes in the preheated oven for 25–30 minutes, or until golden brown and firm to the touch. Transfer to a wire rack and leave to cool. Dust with icing sugar.

MACADAMIA & MAPLE CUPCAKES

Preheat the oven to 190°C/375°F/Gas Mark 5. Put 10 paper bun cases in a bun tin or put 10 double-layer paper cases on a baking tray.

Put the butter, brown sugar and maple syrup in a bowl and beat together until light and fluffy. Gradually beat in the egg. Sift in the flour and, using a metal spoon, fold into the mixture with the nuts and milk. Spoon the mixture into the paper cases.

Bake the cupcakes in the preheated oven for 20 minutes, or until golden brown and firm to the touch. Transfer to a wire rack and leave to cool.

To make the frosting, beat the butter and maple syrup together until smooth. Sift in the icing sugar and beat in thoroughly. Gently beat in the cream cheese. Swirl the icing on the top of the cupcakes and sprinkle over the toasted nuts.

Makes 10

85 g/3 oz butter, softened

55 g/2 oz soft light brown sugar

2 tbsp maple syrup

1 large egg, lightly beaten

85 g/3 oz self-raising flour

55 g/2 oz macadamia nuts, chopped

1 tbsp milk

2 tbsp chopped macadamia nuts, lightly toasted

Frosting

25 g/1 oz butter, softened

2 tbsp maple syrup

85 g/3 oz icing sugar, sifted

85 g/3 oz cream cheese

SPICED PLUM CUPCAKES

Makes 4

55 g/2 oz butter, softened, plus extra for greasing

55 g/2 oz caster sugar

1 large egg, lightly beaten

55 g/2 oz plain wholemeal flour

½ tsp baking powder

1 tsp ground mixed spice

25 g/1 oz blanched hazelnuts, coarsely ground

2 small plums, halved, stoned and sliced

Greek-style yogurt, to serve

Preheat the oven to 180°C/350°F/Gas Mark 4. Grease 4 x 150-ml/5-fl oz ovenproof teacups or ramekins.

Put the butter and sugar in a bowl and beat together until light and fluffy. Gradually beat in the egg. Sift in the flour, baking powder and mixed spice (tipping any bran left in the sieve into the bowl) and, using a metal spoon, fold into the mixture with the ground hazelnuts. Spoon the mixture into the prepared teacups or ramekins. Arrange the sliced plums on top of the mixture.

Put the teacups or ramekins on a baking tray and bake in the preheated oven for 25 minutes, or until risen and firm to the touch. Serve warm or cold with Greek-style yogurt.

LOW-FAT BLUEBERRY MUFFINS

Preheat the oven to 190°C/375°F/Gas Mark 5. Place 12 paper muffin cases in a muffin tin.

Sift the flour, bicarbonate of soda, salt and half the allspice into a large mixing bowl. Add 6 tablespoons of the sugar and mix together well.

In a separate bowl, lightly whisk the egg whites together. Add the margarine, yogurt and vanilla extract and mix well, then stir in the blueberries until thoroughly mixed. Add the fruit mixture to the dry ingredients, then gently stir until just combined. Do not over-mix – it is fine for the mixture to be a little lumpy.

Divide the mixture evenly between the paper cases (they should be about two-thirds full). Mix the remaining sugar with the remaining allspice, then sprinkle the mixture over the muffins.

Bake in the preheated oven for 25 minutes, or until risen and golden. Remove the muffins from the oven and serve warm, or place them on a wire rack to cool completely.

Makes 12

225 g/8 oz plain flour

1 tsp bicarbonate of soda

¼ tsp salt

1 tsp allspice

115 g/4 oz caster sugar

3 large egg whites

3 tbsp low-fat margarine

150 ml/5 fl oz thick low-fat natural yogurt or blueberry-flavoured yogurt

1 tsp vanilla extract

85 g/3 oz fresh blueberries

LEMON & POPPY SEED MUFFINS

Makes 12

350 g/12 oz plain flour

1 tbsp baking powder

115 g/4 oz caster sugar

2 tbsp poppy seeds

55 g/2 oz unsalted butter

1 large egg, beaten

225 ml/8 fl oz milk

finely grated rind and juice of
1 lemon

Preheat the oven to 190°C/375°F/Gas Mark 5. Place
12 paper muffin cases in a muffin tin.

Sift the flour and baking powder into a large bowl and
stir in the sugar.

Heat a heavy-based frying pan over a medium–high
heat and add the poppy seeds, then toast for about
30 seconds, shaking the pan to prevent them from
burning. Remove from the heat and add to the
flour mixture.

Melt the butter, then beat with the egg, milk, lemon rind
and lemon juice. Pour into the dry mixture and stir well to
mix evenly to a soft, sticky dough. Add a little more milk if
the mixture is too dry.

Spoon the mixture into the muffin cases, then bake in
the preheated oven for 25–30 minutes, or until risen and
golden brown. Place on a wire rack to cool.

JAM DOUGHNUT MUFFINS

Preheat the oven to 200°C/400°F/Gas Mark 6. Grease a 12-cup muffin tin or line with 12 paper muffin cases.

Sift together the flour, baking powder and salt into a large bowl. Stir in the caster sugar.

Lightly beat the eggs in a large jug or bowl then beat in the milk, oil and vanilla extract. Make a well in the centre of the dry ingredients and pour in the beaten liquid ingredients. Stir gently until just combined; do not over-mix.

Spoon half of the mixture into the prepared muffin tin. Add a teaspoon of jam to the centre of each, then spoon in the remaining mixture. Bake in the preheated oven for about 20 minutes, until well risen, golden brown and firm to the touch.

Meanwhile, prepare the topping. Melt the butter. Spread the granulated sugar in a wide, shallow bowl. When the muffins are baked, leave in the tin for 5 minutes. Dip the tops of the muffins in the melted butter then roll in the sugar. Serve warm or transfer to a wire rack and leave to cool.

Makes 12

oil or melted butter, for greasing (if using)

280 g/10 oz plain flour

1 tbsp baking powder

1/8 tsp salt

115 g/4 oz caster sugar

2 eggs

200 ml/7 fl oz milk

6 tbsp sunflower oil or 85 g/3 oz butter, melted and cooled

1 tsp vanilla extract

4 tbsp strawberry jam or raspberry jam

Topping

115 g/4 oz butter

150 g/5½ oz granulated sugar

TROPICAL FRUIT MUFFINS

Makes 12

oil or melted butter,
for greasing (if using)

2 bananas

about 150 ml/5 fl oz milk

280 g/10 oz plain flour

1 tbsp baking powder

1/8 tsp salt

115 g/4 oz soft light brown
sugar

2 eggs

6 tbsp sunflower oil or 85 g/3 oz
butter, melted and cooled

1 tsp vanilla extract

2 passion fruits

2 tbsp clear honey

Preheat the oven to 200°C/400°F/Gas Mark 6. Grease
a 12-cup muffin tin or line with 12 paper muffin cases.

Mash the bananas and put in a measuring jug. Make up
the purée to 250 ml/9 fl oz with milk.

Sift together the flour, baking powder and salt into a large
bowl. Stir in the sugar.

Lightly beat the eggs in a large jug or bowl then beat in
the banana and milk mixture, oil and vanilla extract. Make
a well in the centre of the dry ingredients and pour in the
beaten liquid ingredients. Stir gently until just combined;
do not over-mix.

Spoon the mixture into the prepared muffin tin. Bake in
the preheated oven for about 20 minutes, until well risen,
golden brown and firm to the touch.

Leave the muffins in the tin for 5 minutes, then transfer to a
wire rack and leave to cool.

Meanwhile, halve the passion fruits and spoon the pulp
into a small saucepan. Add the honey and heat very
gently until warmed through. Spoon on top of the muffins
before serving.

VICTORIA SPONGE CAKE

Preheat the oven to 180°C/350°F/Gas Mark 4. Grease 2 x 20-cm/8-inch sandwich tins and line with baking paper.

Cream the butter and sugar together in a mixing bowl using a wooden spoon or a hand-held whisk until the mixture is pale in colour and light and fluffy. Add the egg a little at a time, beating well after each addition.

Sift the flour and salt and carefully add to the mixture, folding it in with a metal spoon or a spatula. Divide the mixture between the prepared tins and smooth over with the spatula.

Place on the same shelf in the centre of the preheated oven and bake for 25–30 minutes, until well risen, golden brown and beginning to shrink from the sides of the tin.

Remove from the oven and allow to stand for 1 minute. Loosen the cakes from around the edges of the tins using a palette knife. Turn the cakes out onto a clean tea towel, remove the paper and invert onto a wire rack.

When completely cool, sandwich together with the jam and sprinkle with the sugar.

Serves 8–10

175 g/6 oz butter, softened, plus extra for greasing

175 g/6 oz caster sugar

3 eggs, beaten

175 g/6 oz self-raising flour

pinch of salt

3 tbsp raspberry jam

1 tbsp caster sugar or icing sugar

COFFEE & WALNUT CAKE

Serves 8

175 g/6 oz unsalted butter, plus extra for greasing

175 g/6 oz light muscovado sugar

3 large eggs, beaten

3 tbsp strong black coffee

175 g/6 oz self-raising flour

1½ tsp baking powder

115 g/4 oz walnut pieces

walnut halves, to decorate

Frosting

115 g/4 oz unsalted butter

200 g/7 oz icing sugar

1 tbsp strong black coffee

½ tsp vanilla extract

Preheat the oven to 180°C/350°F/Gas Mark 4. Grease and line the bases of 2 x 20-cm/8-inch sandwich tins.

Cream together the butter and muscovado sugar until pale and fluffy. Gradually add the eggs, beating well after each addition. Beat in the coffee.

Sift the flour and baking powder into the mixture, then fold in lightly and evenly with a metal spoon. Fold in the walnut pieces.

Divide the mixture between the prepared cake tins and smooth level. Bake in the preheated oven for 20–25 minutes, or until golden brown and springy to the touch. Turn out onto a wire rack to cool.

For the frosting, beat together the butter, icing sugar, coffee and vanilla extract, mixing until smooth and creamy.

Use about half the mixture to sandwich the cakes together, then spread the remaining frosting on top and swirl with a palette knife. Decorate with walnut halves.

CLASSIC CHERRY CAKE

Preheat the oven to 180°C/350°F/Gas Mark 4. Grease a 20-cm/8-inch round cake tin and line with baking paper.

Stir together the cherries, ground almonds and 1 tablespoon of the flour. Sift the remaining flour into a separate bowl with the baking powder.

Cream together the butter and sugar until light in colour and fluffy in texture. Gradually add the eggs, beating hard with each addition, until evenly mixed.

Add the flour mixture and fold lightly and evenly into the creamed mixture with a metal spoon. Add the cherry mixture and fold in evenly. Finally, fold in the lemon rind and juice.

Spoon the mixture into the prepared cake tin and sprinkle with the crushed sugar cubes. Bake in the preheated oven for 1–1¼ hours, or until risen, golden brown and the cake is just beginning to shrink away from the sides of the tin.

Cool in the tin for about 15 minutes, then turn out to finish cooling on a wire rack.

Serves 8

250 g/9 oz glacé cherries, quartered

85 g/3 oz ground almonds

200 g/7 oz plain flour

1 tsp baking powder

200 g/7 oz unsalted butter, plus extra for greasing

200 g/7 oz caster sugar

3 large eggs

finely grated rind and juice of 1 lemon

6 sugar cubes, crushed

JEWEL-TOPPED MADEIRA CAKE

Serves 8–10

225 g/8 oz butter, softened, plus extra for greasing

225 g/8 oz golden caster sugar

finely grated rind of 1 lemon

4 eggs, beaten

350 g/12 oz self-raising flour, sifted

2–3 tbsp milk

Fruit topping

2½ tbsp honey

300 g/10½ oz glacé fruit, sliced

Preheat the oven to 160°C/325°F/Gas Mark 3. Grease a 20-cm/8-inch round deep cake tin and line with baking paper.

Put the butter, sugar and lemon rind in a bowl and beat together until light and fluffy. Gradually beat in the eggs. Gently fold in the flour, adding enough milk to give a soft dropping consistency.

Spoon the mixture into the prepared tin and bake in the preheated oven for 1½–1¾ hours, until risen and golden and a skewer inserted into the centre comes out clean.

Leave in the tin for 10 minutes, then turn out, remove the paper and place on a wire rack to cool. To make the topping, brush the honey over the cake and arrange the fruit on top.

PINEAPPLE UPSIDE-DOWN CAKE

Preheat the oven to 160°C/325°F/Gas Mark 3. Grease a 23-cm/9-inch round deep tin with a solid base and line the base with baking paper.

For the topping, place the butter and golden syrup in a heavy-based saucepan and heat gently until melted. Bring to the boil and boil for 2–3 minutes, stirring, until slightly thickened and toffee-like.

Pour the syrup into the base of the prepared tin. Arrange the pineapple rings and glacé cherries in one layer over the syrup.

Place the eggs, sugar and vanilla extract in a large heatproof bowl over a saucepan of gently simmering water and whisk with an electric mixer for about 10–15 minutes, until thick enough to leave a trail when the whisk is lifted. Sift in the flour and baking powder and fold in lightly and evenly with a metal spoon.

Fold the melted butter into the mixture with a metal spoon until evenly mixed. Spoon into the prepared tin and bake in the preheated oven for 1–1¼ hours, or until well risen, firm and golden brown.

Leave to cool in the tin for 10 minutes, then carefully turn out onto a serving plate. Serve warm or cold.

Serves 10
4 eggs, beaten

200 g/7 oz golden caster sugar

1 tsp vanilla extract

200 g/7 oz plain flour

2 tsp baking powder

125 g/4½ oz unsalted butter, melted, plus extra for greasing

Topping
40 g/1½ oz unsalted butter

4 tbsp golden syrup

425 g/15 oz canned pineapple rings, drained

4–6 glacé cherries, halved

APPLE STREUSEL CAKE

Serves 8

500 g/1 lb 2 oz eating apples, peeled, cored and cut into 1-cm/½-inch dice

1 tbsp lemon juice

125 g/4½ oz unsalted butter, plus extra for greasing

125 g/4½ oz golden caster sugar

2 large eggs, beaten

225 g/8 oz plain flour

3 tsp baking powder

1 tsp ground cinnamon

½ tsp ground nutmeg

3 tbsp cider or apple juice

Streusel topping

40 g/1½ oz hazelnuts, skinned and finely chopped

40 g/1½ oz plain flour

25 g/1 oz light muscovado sugar

½ tsp ground cinnamon

25 g/1 oz unsalted butter, melted

Preheat the oven to 180°C/350°F/Gas Mark 4. Grease a 20-cm/8-inch round loose-based cake tin and line the base with baking paper. Toss the apples in the lemon juice.

Cream together the butter and caster sugar until pale and fluffy, then gradually add the eggs, beating thoroughly after each addition. Sift the flour, baking powder, cinnamon and nutmeg into the mixture and fold in lightly and evenly using a metal spoon. Stir in the cider.

Stir the apples into the mixture to distribute evenly, then spoon into the prepared tin and level the surface.

For the streusel topping, mix together the hazelnuts, flour, muscovado sugar and cinnamon, then stir in the melted butter, mixing until crumbly. Spread over the cake.

Bake the cake in the preheated oven for 1–1¼ hours, or until firm and golden brown. Cool for 10 minutes in the tin, then remove carefully and finish cooling on a wire rack.

HONEY & ALMOND CAKE

Preheat the oven to 180°C/350°F/Gas Mark 4. Grease an 18-cm/7-inch round cake tin and line with baking paper.

Place the margarine, sugar, eggs, flour, baking powder, milk and honey in a large mixing bowl and beat well with a wooden spoon for about 1 minute, or until all of the ingredients are thoroughly mixed together.

Spoon into the prepared tin, smooth the surface with the back of a spoon or a knife and sprinkle with the almonds.

Bake in the preheated oven for about 50 minutes, or until well risen and a skewer inserted into the centre comes out clean.

Meanwhile, make the syrup. Combine the honey and lemon juice in a small saucepan and simmer over a low heat for about 5 minutes, or until the syrup coats the back of a spoon.

As soon as the cake comes out of the oven, pour the syrup over it, letting it soak into the cake.

Leave the cake to cool in the tin for at least 2 hours before slicing.

Serves 8

75 g/2¾ oz soft margarine, plus extra for greasing

75 g/2¾ oz soft light brown sugar

2 eggs

175 g/6 oz self-raising flour

1 tsp baking powder

4 tbsp milk

2 tbsp clear honey

50 g/1¾ oz flaked almonds

Syrup

225 g/8 oz honey

2 tbsp lemon juice

BANANA & CRANBERRY LOAF

Serves 8–10

butter, for greasing

175 g/6 oz self-raising flour

½ tsp baking powder

150 g/5½ oz soft light brown sugar

2 bananas, mashed

50 g/1¾ oz chopped mixed peel

25 g/1 oz chopped mixed nuts

50 g/1¾ oz dried cranberries

5–6 tbsp orange juice

2 eggs, beaten

150 ml/5 fl oz sunflower oil

75 g/2¾ oz icing sugar, sifted

grated rind of 1 orange

Preheat the oven to 180°C/350°F/Gas Mark 4. Grease a 900-g/2-lb loaf tin and line with baking paper.

Sift the flour and baking powder into a mixing bowl. Stir in the sugar, bananas, mixed peel, nuts and cranberries.

Mix the orange juice, eggs and oil together in a separate bowl until well combined. Add to the dry ingredients and mix until well blended. Pour the mixture into the prepared tin.

Bake in the preheated oven for about 1 hour, until firm to the touch and a skewer inserted into the centre comes out clean. Turn out onto a wire rack to cool.

Mix the icing sugar with a little water and drizzle the icing over the loaf. Sprinkle over the orange rind and leave the icing to set before serving.

ORANGE & POPPY SEED BUNDT CAKE

Preheat the oven to 160°C/325°F/Gas Mark 3. Grease and lightly flour a Bundt ring tin, about 24 cm/9½ inches in diameter and with a capacity of approximately 2 litres/3½ pints.

Cream together the butter and sugar until pale and fluffy, then add the eggs gradually, beating thoroughly after each addition. Stir in the orange rind and poppy seeds. Sift in the flour and baking powder, then fold in evenly. Add the milk and orange juice, stirring to mix evenly.

Spoon the mixture into the prepared tin and bake in the preheated oven for 45–50 minutes, or until firm and golden brown. Leave to cool in the tin for 10 minutes, then turn out onto a wire rack to cool.

For the syrup, place the sugar and orange juice in a saucepan and heat gently until the sugar melts. Bring to the boil and simmer for about 5 minutes, until reduced and syrupy.

Spoon the syrup over the cake whilst it is still warm. Top with the strips of orange zest and serve warm or cold.

Serves 10

200 g/7 oz unsalted butter, plus extra for greasing

200 g/7 oz golden caster sugar

3 large eggs, beaten

finely grated rind of 1 orange

55 g/2 oz poppy seeds

300 g/10½ oz plain flour, plus extra for dusting

2 tsp baking powder

150 ml/5 fl oz milk

125 ml/4 fl oz orange juice

strips of orange zest, to decorate

Syrup

140 g/5 oz golden caster sugar

150 ml/5 fl oz orange juice

GLOSSY FRUIT LOAF

Serves 10

55 g/2 oz raisins

85 g/3 oz dried apricots, roughly chopped

55 g/2 oz stoned dates, chopped

90 ml/3 fl oz cold black tea

115 g/4 oz butter, plus extra for greasing

115 g/4 oz light muscovado sugar

2 eggs, beaten

175 g/6 oz self-raising flour, sifted

55 g/2 oz glacé pineapple, roughly chopped

85 g/3 oz glacé cherries, halved

85 g/3 oz Brazil nuts, roughly chopped

Topping

walnut halves

whole Brazil nuts

glacé cherries, halved

2 tbsp apricot jam, sieved

Place the raisins, apricots and dates in a bowl, pour over the tea and leave to soak for 8 hours, or overnight.

Preheat the oven to 160°C/325°F/Gas Mark 3. Grease and line a 900-g/2-lb loaf tin.

Beat the butter and sugar together until light and fluffy. Gradually beat in the eggs, then fold in the flour alternately with the soaked fruit. Gently stir in the glacé pineapple, glacé cherries and chopped Brazil nuts. Spoon the mixture into the prepared tin. For the topping, arrange the walnut halves, whole Brazil nuts and glacé cherry halves over the surface.

Bake in the preheated oven for 1½–1¾ hours, or until a skewer inserted into the centre comes out clean. Leave to cool in the tin for 10 minutes, then turn out and peel off the lining paper. Transfer to a wire rack to cool completely. Warm the apricot jam in a small saucepan over a low heat and brush over the top of the cake.

DATE & WALNUT TEABREAD

Preheat the oven to 180°C/350°F/Gas Mark 4. Grease a 450-g/1-lb loaf tin and line the base with baking paper.

Place the dates, bicarbonate of soda and lemon rind in a bowl and add the hot tea. Leave to soak for 10 minutes, until soft.

Cream together the butter and sugar until light and fluffy, then beat in the egg. Stir in the date mixture.

Fold in the flour using a large metal spoon, then fold in the chopped walnuts. Spoon the mixture into the prepared loaf tin and spread evenly. Top with walnut halves.

Bake in the preheated oven for 35–40 minutes, or until risen, firm and golden brown. Cool for 10 minutes in the tin, then turn out the loaf and finish cooling on a wire rack.

Serves 8

100 g/3½ oz stoned dates, chopped

½ tsp bicarbonate of soda

finely grated rind of ½ lemon

100 ml/3½ fl oz hot tea

40 g/1½ oz unsalted butter, plus extra for greasing

70 g/2½ oz light muscovado sugar

1 small egg

125 g/4½ oz self-raising flour

25 g/1 oz walnuts, chopped

walnut halves, to decorate

BLACKBERRY & APPLE LOAF

Serves 10

butter, for greasing

350 g/12 oz cooking apples

3 tbsp lemon juice

350 g/12 oz self-raising wholemeal flour

½ tsp baking powder

1 tsp ground cinnamon, plus extra for dusting

115 g/4 oz prepared blackberries, thawed, if frozen

115 g/4 oz light muscovado sugar

1 egg, beaten

200 ml/7 fl oz low-fat natural yogurt

55 g/2 oz white or brown sugar lumps, lightly crushed

Preheat the oven to 190°C/375°F/Gas Mark 5. Grease and line a 900-g/2-lb loaf tin.

Peel, core and finely dice the apples. Place them in a saucepan with the lemon juice, bring to the boil, cover and simmer for about 10 minutes, until soft and pulpy. Beat well and set aside to cool.

Sift the flour, baking powder and cinnamon into a bowl, adding any husks that remain in the sieve. Stir in 70 g/2½ oz of the blackberries and the sugar.

Make a well in the centre of the ingredients and add the egg, yogurt and cooled apple purée. Mix well to incorporate thoroughly. Spoon the mixture into the prepared tin and smooth the top.

Sprinkle with the remaining blackberries, pressing them down into the cake mixture, and top with the crushed sugar lumps. Bake in the preheated oven for 40–45 minutes. Remove from the oven and set aside in the tin to cool.

Remove the cake from the tin and peel away the lining paper. Serve dusted with cinnamon.

FROSTED CARROT CAKE

Preheat the oven to 180°C/350°F/Gas Mark 4. Grease and line the base of a 23-cm/9-inch square cake tin.

In a large bowl beat together the oil, muscovado sugar and eggs. Stir in the grated carrots, sultanas, walnuts and orange rind.

Sift together the flour, bicarbonate of soda, cinnamon and nutmeg, then stir evenly into the carrot mixture.

Spoon the mixture into the prepared cake tin and bake in the preheated oven for 40–45 minutes, until well risen and firm to the touch.

Remove the cake from the oven and set on a wire rack for 5 minutes. Turn out onto the wire rack to cool completely.

For the frosting, combine the soft cheese, icing sugar and orange juice in a bowl and beat until smooth. Spread over the top of the cake and swirl with a palette knife. Decorate with strips of orange zest and serve cut into squares.

Serves 16

175 ml/6 fl oz sunflower oil, plus extra for greasing
175 g/6 oz light muscovado sugar
3 eggs, beaten
175 g/6 oz grated carrots
85 g/3 oz sultanas
55 g/2 oz walnut pieces
grated rind of 1 orange
175 g/6 oz self-raising flour
1 tsp bicarbonate of soda
1 tsp ground cinnamon
½ tsp grated nutmeg
strips of orange zest, to decorate

Frosting
200 g/7 oz full-fat soft cheese
100 g/3½ oz icing sugar
2 tsp orange juice

HUMMINGBIRD CAKE

Serves 10

250 g/9 oz plain flour

250 g/9 oz caster sugar

1 tsp ground cinnamon

1 tsp bicarbonate of soda

3 eggs, beaten

200 ml/7 fl oz sunflower oil, plus extra for greasing

100 g/3½ oz pecan nuts, roughly chopped, plus extra to decorate

3 ripe bananas (about 375 g/ 13 oz peeled weight), mashed

85 g/3 oz canned crushed pineapple (drained weight), plus 4 tbsp juice from the can

Frosting

175 g/6 oz full-fat soft cheese

55 g/2 oz unsalted butter

1 tsp vanilla extract

400 g/14 oz icing sugar

Preheat the oven to 180°C/350°F/Gas Mark 4. Lightly grease 3 x 23-cm/9-inch sandwich tins with oil and line the bases with baking paper.

Sift together the flour, caster sugar, cinnamon and bicarbonate of soda into a large bowl. Add the eggs, oil, pecan nuts, bananas, pineapple and pineapple juice, and stir with a wooden spoon until evenly mixed.

Divide the mixture between the prepared tins, spreading evenly. Bake in the preheated oven for 25–30 minutes, or until golden brown and firm to the touch.

Remove the cakes from the oven and leave to cool for 10 minutes in the tins before turning out onto wire racks to cool.

For the frosting, beat together the soft cheese, butter and vanilla extract in a bowl until smooth. Sift in the icing sugar and mix until smooth.

Sandwich the cakes together with half of the frosting, spread the remaining frosting over the top, then sprinkle with chopped pecan nuts to decorate.

RED VELVET CAKE

Preheat the oven to 190°C/375°F/Gas Mark 5. Grease 2 x 23-cm/9-inch sandwich tins and line the bases with baking paper.

Place the butter, water and cocoa powder in a small saucepan and heat gently, without boiling, stirring until melted and smooth. Remove from the heat and leave to cool slightly.

Beat together the eggs, buttermilk, vanilla extract and food colouring until frothy. Beat in the butter mixture. Sift in the flour, cornflour and baking powder, then stir quickly and evenly into the mixture with the caster sugar.

Divide the mixture between the prepared tins and bake in the preheated oven for 25–30 minutes, or until risen and firm to the touch. Leave to cool in the tins for 3–4 minutes, then turn out and finish cooling on a wire rack.

For the frosting, beat together all the ingredients until smooth. Use about half of the frosting to sandwich the cakes together, then spread the remainder over the top, swirling with a palette knife.

*If you prefer not to use synthetic food colouring, this can be replaced by 4 tablespoons of beetroot juice: you should reduce the water quantity to 2 tablespoons.

Serves 12

225 g/8 oz unsalted butter, plus extra for greasing
4 tbsp water
55 g/2 oz cocoa powder
3 eggs
250 ml/9 fl oz buttermilk
2 tsp vanilla extract
2 tbsp red edible food colouring*
280 g/10 oz plain flour
55 g/2 oz cornflour
1½ tsp baking powder
280 g/10 oz caster sugar

Frosting

250 g/9 oz full-fat soft cheese
40 g/1½ oz unsalted butter
3 tbsp caster sugar
1 tsp vanilla extract

COCONUT BARS

Makes 10

125 g/4½ oz unsalted butter, plus extra for greasing

225 g/8 oz golden caster sugar

2 eggs, beaten

finely grated rind of 1 orange

3 tbsp orange juice

150 ml/5 fl oz soured cream

140 g/5 oz self-raising flour

85 g/3 oz desiccated coconut

toasted shredded coconut, to decorate

Frosting

1 egg white

200 g/7 oz icing sugar

85 g/3 oz desiccated coconut

about 1 tbsp orange juice

Preheat the oven to 180°C/350°F/Gas Mark 4. Grease a 23-cm/9-inch square cake tin and line the base with baking paper.

Cream together the butter and caster sugar until pale and fluffy, then gradually beat in the eggs. Stir in the orange rind, orange juice and soured cream. Fold in the flour and desiccated coconut evenly using a metal spoon.

Spoon the mixture into the prepared cake tin and level the surface. Bake in the preheated oven for 35–40 minutes, or until risen and firm to the touch.

Leave to cool for 10 minutes in the tin, then turn out and finish cooling on a wire rack.

For the frosting, lightly beat the egg white, just enough to break it up, and stir in the icing sugar and desiccated coconut, adding enough orange juice to mix to a thick paste. Spread over the top of the cake, sprinkle with toasted shredded coconut, then leave to set before slicing into bars.

LEMON DRIZZLE BARS

Preheat the oven to 180°C/350°F/Gas Mark 4. Grease an 18-cm/7-inch square cake tin and line with baking paper.

Place the eggs, caster sugar and margarine in a mixing bowl and beat hard until smooth and fluffy. Stir in the lemon rind, then fold in the flour lightly and evenly. Stir in the milk, mixing evenly, then spoon into the prepared cake tin, smoothing level.

Bake in the preheated oven for 45–50 minutes, or until golden brown and firm to the touch. Remove from the oven and stand the tin on a wire rack.

To make the syrup, place the icing sugar and lemon juice in a small saucepan and heat gently, stirring until the sugar dissolves. Do not boil.

Prick the warm cake all over with a skewer and spoon the hot syrup evenly over the top, allowing it to be absorbed.

Leave to cool completely in the tin, then turn out the cake, cut into 12 pieces and dust with a little icing sugar before serving.

Makes 12

2 eggs

175 g/6 oz caster sugar

150 g/5½ oz soft margarine, plus extra for greasing

finely grated rind of 1 lemon

175 g/6 oz self-raising flour

125 ml/4 fl oz milk

icing sugar, for dusting

Syrup

140 g/5 oz icing sugar

50 ml/2 fl oz freshly squeezed lemon juice

TOFFEE APPLE SQUARES

Makes 9

115 g/4 oz unsalted butter, plus extra for greasing

175 g/6 oz light muscovado sugar

2 eggs, beaten

200 g/7 oz plain flour

1 tsp baking powder

½ tsp bicarbonate of soda

1½ tsp ground mixed spice

2 eating apples, peeled and coarsely grated

85 g/3 oz hazelnuts, chopped

Toffee apple topping

85 g/3 oz light muscovado sugar

55 g/2 oz unsalted butter

1 eating apple, cored and thinly sliced

Preheat the oven to 180°C/350°F/Gas Mark 4. Grease a 23-cm/9-inch square shallow cake tin.

For the topping, place the sugar and butter in a small pan and heat gently, stirring, until melted. Pour into the prepared tin. Arrange the apple slices over the mixture.

Place the butter and sugar in a bowl and beat well until pale and fluffy. Beat in the eggs gradually.

Sift in the flour, baking powder, bicarbonate of soda and mixed spice, and fold into the mixture. Stir in the grated apples and hazelnuts.

Pour into the prepared tin and bake in the preheated oven for 35–40 minutes, until firm and golden. Cool in the tin for 10 minutes, then turn out and cut into squares.

CRUNCHY

Deliciously moreish cookies

CHOCOLATE CHIP COOKIES

Preheat the oven to 190°C/375°F/Gas Mark 5. Lightly grease 2 baking trays.

Place all of the ingredients in a large mixing bowl and beat until well combined.

Place tablespoonfuls of the mixture onto the prepared baking trays, spacing them well apart to allow for spreading during cooking.

Bake in the preheated oven for 10–12 minutes, or until the cookies are golden brown.

Using a palette knife, transfer the cookies to a wire rack to cool completely.

Makes 30

175 g/6 oz plain flour

1 tsp baking powder

125 g/4½ oz soft margarine, plus extra for greasing

85 g/3 oz light muscovado sugar

55 g/2 oz caster sugar

½ tsp vanilla extract

1 egg

125 g/4½ oz plain chocolate chips

CLASSIC OAT COOKIES

Makes 30

175 g/6 oz butter or margarine, plus extra for greasing

275 g/9¾ oz demerara sugar

1 egg

4 tbsp water

1 tsp vanilla extract

375 g/13 oz rolled oats

140 g/5 oz plain flour

1 tsp salt

½ tsp bicarbonate of soda

Preheat the oven to 350°F/180°C/Gas Mark 4 and grease a large baking tray.

Cream the butter and sugar together in a large mixing bowl. Beat in the egg, water and vanilla extract until the mixture is smooth. In a separate bowl, mix the oats, flour, salt and bicarbonate of soda.

Gradually stir the oat mixture into the creamed mixture until thoroughly combined.

Place tablespoonfuls of the mixture onto the prepared baking tray, making sure they are well spaced. Transfer to the preheated oven and bake for 15 minutes, or until the cookies are golden brown.

Remove the cookies from the oven and place on a wire rack to cool before serving.

CHEWY GOLDEN COOKIES

Preheat the oven to 180°C/350°F/Gas Mark 4. Grease a large baking tray and line with baking paper.

In a large mixing bowl, blend the butter, sugar, golden syrup and egg whites together. Gradually add the oats, flour, salt and baking powder and mix thoroughly.

Drop 30 rounded tablespoonfuls of the mixture onto the prepared baking tray. Bake in the preheated oven for 12 minutes, or until the cookies are light brown.

Remove from the oven and transfer to a wire rack to cool. Mix the icing sugar with a few drops of water to form a thin icing, drizzle over the cookies and leave to set.

Makes 30

175 g/6 oz butter or margarine, plus extra for greasing

250 g/9 oz soft light brown sugar

350 g/12 oz golden syrup

3 egg whites

250 g/9 oz rolled oats

280 g/10 oz plain flour

pinch of salt

1 tsp baking powder

2 tbsp icing sugar

OAT, RAISIN & NUT COOKIES

Makes about 30

55 g/2 oz raisins, chopped
125 ml/4 fl oz orange juice
225 g/8 oz butter, softened
140 g/5 oz caster sugar
1 egg yolk, lightly beaten
2 tsp vanilla extract
225 g/8 oz plain flour
a pinch of salt
55 g/2 oz rolled oats
55 g/2 oz hazelnuts, chopped
whole hazelnuts, to decorate

Preheat the oven to 190°C/375°F/Gas Mark 5. Line 2 baking trays with baking paper.

Put the raisins in a bowl, add the orange juice and leave to soak for 10 minutes.

Put the butter and sugar into a bowl and mix well with a wooden spoon, then beat in the egg yolk and vanilla extract. Sift together the flour and salt into the mixture and add the oats and hazelnuts. Drain the raisins, add them to the mixture and stir until thoroughly combined.

Scoop up tablespoons of the mixture and place them in mounds on the prepared baking trays, spaced well apart. Flatten slightly and place a whole hazelnut in the centre of each cookie.

Bake in the preheated oven for 12–15 minutes, until golden brown. Leave to cool on the baking trays for 5–10 minutes, then carefully transfer the cookies to wire racks to cool completely.

STICKY GINGER COOKIES

Put the butter and sugar into a bowl and mix well with a wooden spoon, then beat in the egg yolk and ginger syrup. Sift together the flour and salt into the mixture, add the stem ginger and chocolate chips and stir until thoroughly combined.

Shape the mixture into a log, wrap in clingfilm and chill in the refrigerator for 30–60 minutes.

Preheat the oven to 190°C/375°F/Gas Mark 5. Line 2 baking trays with baking paper.

Unwrap the log and cut it into 5-mm/¼-inch slices with a sharp serrated knife. Put them onto the prepared baking trays, spaced well apart.

Bake in the preheated oven for 12–15 minutes, until golden brown. Leave to cool on the baking trays for 5–10 minutes, then carefully transfer the cookies to wire racks to cool completely.

Makes 20

225 g/8 oz butter, softened

140 g/5 oz golden caster sugar

1 egg yolk, lightly beaten

55 g/2 oz stem ginger, coarsely chopped, plus 1 tbsp syrup from the jar

280 g/10 oz plain flour

pinch of salt

55 g/2 oz plain chocolate chips

APRICOT & PECAN COOKIES

Makes about 30

225 g/8 oz butter, softened

140 g/5 oz caster sugar

1 egg yolk, lightly beaten

2 tsp vanilla extract

280 g/10 oz plain flour

pinch of salt

grated rind of 1 orange

55 g/2 oz ready-to-eat dried apricots, chopped

100 g/3½ oz pecan nuts, finely chopped

Put the butter and sugar into a bowl and mix well with a wooden spoon, then beat in the egg yolk and vanilla extract. Sift together the flour and salt into the mixture, add the orange rind and apricots and stir until thoroughly combined.

Shape the dough into a log. Spread out the pecan nuts in a shallow dish. Roll the log in the nuts until well coated, then wrap in clingfilm and chill in the refrigerator for 30–60 minutes.

Preheat the oven to 190°C/375°F/Gas Mark 5. Line 2 baking trays with baking paper.

Unwrap the dough and cut into 5-mm/¼-inch slices with a sharp serrated knife. Put the slices onto the prepared baking trays, spaced well apart.

Bake in the preheated oven for 10–12 minutes. Leave to cool on the baking trays for 5–10 minutes, then carefully transfer to wire racks to cool completely.

PEANUT BUTTER COOKIES

Preheat the oven to 180°C/350°F/Gas Mark 4, then grease 3 baking trays.

Place the butter and peanut butter in a bowl and beat together. Beat in the caster sugar and muscovado sugar, then gradually beat in the egg and the vanilla extract.

Sift the flour, bicarbonate of soda, baking powder and salt into the mixture, add the oats and stir until just combined.

Place spoonfuls of the mixture onto the prepared baking trays, spaced well apart to allow for spreading. Flatten slightly with a fork.

Bake in the preheated oven for 12 minutes, or until lightly browned. Leave to cool on the baking trays for 2 minutes, then transfer to wire racks to cool completely.

Makes 26

115 g/4 oz butter, softened, plus extra for greasing
115 g/4 oz crunchy peanut butter
115 g/4 oz golden caster sugar
115 g/4 oz light muscovado sugar
1 egg, beaten
½ tsp vanilla extract
85 g/3 oz plain flour
½ tsp bicarbonate of soda
½ tsp baking powder
pinch of salt
115 g/4 oz rolled oats

BANANA & RAISIN COOKIES

Makes about 30

25 g/1 oz raisins

125 ml/4 fl oz orange juice or rum

225 g/8 oz butter, softened

140 g/5 oz caster sugar

1 egg yolk, lightly beaten

280 g/10 oz plain flour

pinch of salt

85 g/3 oz dried bananas, finely chopped

Put the raisins into a bowl, pour in the orange juice and leave to soak for 30 minutes. Drain the raisins, reserving any remaining orange juice.

Preheat the oven to 190°C/375°F/Gas Mark 5. Line 2 baking trays with baking paper.

Put the butter and sugar into a bowl and mix well with a wooden spoon, then beat in the egg yolk and 2 teaspoons of the reserved orange juice. Sift together the flour and salt into the mixture, add the raisins and dried bananas and stir until thoroughly combined.

Put tablespoons of the mixture into heaps on the prepared baking trays, spaced well apart, then flatten them gently. Bake in the preheated oven for 12–15 minutes, until golden. Leave to cool on the baking trays for 5–10 minutes, then carefully transfer to wire racks to cool completely.

GINGERSNAPS

Preheat the oven to 160°C/325°F/Gas Mark 3, then lightly grease several baking trays.

Sift together the flour, salt, sugar, ginger and bicarbonate of soda into a large mixing bowl.

Heat the butter and golden syrup in a saucepan over a very low heat until the butter has melted. Remove the pan from the heat and leave to cool slightly, then pour the contents onto the dry ingredients.

Add the egg and orange rind and mix thoroughly to form a dough. Using your hands, carefully shape the dough into 30 equal-sized balls.

Place the balls, spaced well apart, on the prepared baking trays, then flatten them slightly with your fingers.

Bake in the preheated oven for 15–20 minutes, then carefully transfer to a wire rack to cool.

Makes 30

350 g/12 oz self-raising flour

pinch of salt

200 g/7 oz caster sugar

1 tbsp ground ginger

1 tsp bicarbonate of soda

125 g/4½ oz butter, plus extra for greasing

75 g/2¾ oz golden syrup

1 egg, beaten

1 tsp grated orange rind

WALNUT & COFFEE COOKIES

Makes about 30

2 sachets instant latte powder

1 tbsp hot water

225 g/8 oz butter, softened

140 g/5 oz caster sugar

1 egg yolk, lightly beaten

280 g/10 oz plain flour

pinch of salt

100 g/3½ oz walnuts, finely chopped

coffee sugar crystals, for sprinkling

Put the latte powder into a bowl and stir in the hot water to make a paste. Put the butter and sugar into a bowl and mix well with a wooden spoon, then beat in the egg yolk and coffee paste. Sift the flour and salt into the mixture, add the walnuts and stir until thoroughly combined. Halve the dough, wrap in clingfilm and chill in the refrigerator for 30–60 minutes.

Preheat the oven to 190°C/375°F/Gas Mark 5. Line 2 baking trays with baking paper.

Unwrap the dough and roll out between 2 sheets of baking paper to about 3 mm/⅛ inch thick. Stamp out rounds with a 6 cm/2½-inch cutter and put them onto the prepared baking trays, spaced well apart.

Lightly brush the cookies with water, sprinkle with the coffee sugar crystals and bake in the preheated oven for 10–12 minutes. Leave to cool on the baking trays for 5–10 minutes, then carefully transfer the cookies to wire racks to cool completely.

CITRUS CRESCENTS

Preheat the oven to 200°C/400°F/Gas Mark 6. Lightly grease 2 baking trays.

In a mixing bowl, cream together the butter and sugar until light and fluffy, then gradually beat in the egg yolk.

Sift the flour into the creamed mixture and mix until evenly combined. Add the orange, lemon and lime rinds to the mixture with enough of the orange juice to make a soft dough.

Roll out the dough on a lightly floured surface. Stamp out rounds using a 7.5-cm/3-inch biscuit cutter. Make crescent shapes by cutting away a quarter of each round. Re-roll the trimmings to make about 25 crescents in total.

Place the crescents onto the prepared baking trays. Prick the surface of each crescent with a fork. Lightly whisk the egg white in a small bowl and brush it over the biscuits.

Bake in the preheated oven for 12–15 minutes. Leave the biscuits to cool on a wire rack before serving.

Makes about 25

100 g/3½ oz butter, softened, plus extra for greasing

75 g/2¾ oz caster sugar

1 egg, separated

200 g/7 oz plain flour, plus extra for dusting

grated rind of 1 orange

grated rind of 1 lemon

grated rind of 1 lime

2–3 tbsp orange juice

FLOWER GEMS

Makes about 30

225 g/8 oz butter, softened

140 g/5 oz caster sugar

1 egg yolk, lightly beaten

1 tsp lemon juice

280 g/10 oz plain flour

pinch of salt

2 tbsp jasmine tea leaves

orange, pink, blue and yellow sugar flowers, to decorate

Icing

1 tbsp lemon juice

1 tbsp water

about 200 g/7 oz icing sugar

orange, pink, blue and yellow food colouring

Put the butter and sugar into a bowl and mix well with a wooden spoon, then beat in the egg yolk and lemon juice. Sift together the flour and salt into the mixture, add the tea leaves and stir until thoroughly combined. Halve the dough, wrap in clingfilm and chill in the refrigerator for 30–60 minutes.

Preheat the oven to 190°C/375°F/Gas Mark 5. Line 2 baking trays with baking paper.

Roll out the dough between 2 sheets of baking paper to about 3 mm/⅛ inch thick. Stamp out flower shapes with a 5-cm/2-inch flower-shaped cutter. Put them onto the prepared baking trays, spaced well apart.

Bake in the preheated oven for 10–12 minutes, until golden brown. Leave to cool on the baking trays for 5–10 minutes, then carefully transfer the cookies to wire racks to cool completely.

For the icing, mix the lemon juice with the water in a bowl, then gradually stir in enough of the icing sugar to make a mixture with the consistency of thick cream. Divide the icing among 4 separate bowls and add a drop of different food colouring to each.

Leave the cookies on the racks. Spread orange icing on a quarter of the cookies, pink on another quarter and so on. When the icing is beginning to set, add a matching sugar flower to the centre of each to decorate. Leave to set completely.

VANILLA HEARTS

Preheat the oven to 180°C/350°F/Gas Mark 4, then lightly grease a baking tray.

Sift the flour into a large bowl. Add the butter and rub it in with your fingertips until the mixture resembles fine breadcrumbs. Stir in the sugar and vanilla extract and mix together to form a firm dough.

Roll out the dough on a lightly floured work surface to a thickness of 1 cm/½ inch. Stamp out 12 hearts with a heart-shaped cutter measuring about 5 cm/2 inches across. Arrange the hearts on the prepared baking tray.

Bake in the preheated oven for 15–20 minutes, or until just coloured. Transfer to a wire rack and leave to cool completely. Dust with a little caster sugar just before serving.

Makes 12

225 g/8 oz plain flour, plus extra for dusting

150 g/5½ oz butter, cut into small pieces, plus extra for greasing

125 g/4½ oz caster sugar, plus extra for dusting

1 tsp vanilla extract

JAM RINGS

Makes about 15

225 g/8 oz butter, softened

140 g/5 oz caster sugar, plus extra for sprinkling

1 egg yolk, lightly beaten

2 tsp vanilla extract

280 g/10 oz plain flour

pinch of salt

1 egg white, lightly beaten

Filling

55 g/2 oz butter, softened

100 g/3½ oz icing sugar

5 tbsp strawberry or raspberry jam, warmed

Put the butter and caster sugar into a bowl and mix well with a wooden spoon, then beat in the egg yolk and vanilla extract. Sift the flour and salt into the mixture and stir until thoroughly combined. Halve the dough, wrap in clingfilm and chill in the refrigerator for 30–60 minutes.

Preheat the oven to 190°C/375°F/Gas Mark 5. Line 2 baking trays with baking paper.

Unwrap the dough and roll out between 2 sheets of baking paper. Stamp out 30 biscuits using a 7-cm/ 2¾ inch fluted round cutter and put half of them on 1 of the prepared baking trays, spaced well apart. Using a 4-cm/1½-inch plain round cutter, stamp out the centres of the remaining biscuits and remove. Put the rings on the other baking tray, spaced well apart.

Bake in the preheated oven for 7 minutes, then brush the biscuit rings with beaten egg white and sprinkle with caster sugar. Bake for a further 5–8 minutes, until light golden brown. Leave to cool on the baking trays for 5–10 minutes, then carefully transfer to wire racks to cool completely

To make the filling, beat the butter and icing sugar together in a bowl until smooth and combined. Spread the filling over the whole biscuits and top with a little jam. Place the rings on top and press gently together.

GINGERBREAD PEOPLE

Preheat the oven to 160°C/325°F/Gas Mark 3, then grease 3 large baking trays.

Sift the flour, ginger, mixed spice and bicarbonate of soda into a large bowl. Place the butter, golden syrup and muscovado sugar in a saucepan over a low heat and stir until melted. Pour onto the dry ingredients and add the egg. Mix together to make a dough. The dough will be sticky to start with, but will become firmer as it cools.

On a lightly floured work surface, roll out the dough to about 3 mm/⅛ inch thick and stamp out gingerbread people shapes. Place on the prepared baking trays. Re-knead and re-roll the trimmings and cut out more shapes. Decorate with currants for eyes and pieces of glacé cherry for mouths. Bake in the preheated oven for 15–20 minutes, or until firm and lightly browned.

Remove from the oven and leave to cool on the baking trays for a few minutes, then transfer to wire racks to cool completely.

Mix the icing sugar with the water to a thick consistency. Place the icing in a small piping bag fitted with a plain nozzle and use to pipe buttons or bows onto the cooled biscuits.

Makes 20

450 g/1 lb plain flour, plus extra for dusting

2 tsp ground ginger

1 tsp mixed spice

2 tsp bicarbonate of soda

115 g/4 oz butter, plus extra for greasing

100 g/3½ oz golden syrup

115 g/4 oz light muscovado sugar

1 egg, beaten

To decorate

currants

pieces of glacé cherry

85 g/3 oz icing sugar

3–4 tsp water

CHEQUERBOARD COOKIES

Makes about 20

225 g/8 oz butter, softened
140 g/5 oz caster sugar
1 egg yolk, lightly beaten
2 tsp vanilla extract
280 g/10 oz plain flour
pinch of salt
1 tsp ground ginger
1 tbsp finely grated orange rind
1 tbsp cocoa powder, sifted
1 egg white, lightly beaten

Put the butter and sugar into a bowl and mix well with a wooden spoon, then beat in the egg yolk and vanilla extract. Sift together the flour and salt into the mixture and stir until thoroughly combined.

Divide the dough in half. Add the ginger and orange rind to 1 half and mix well. Shape the dough into a log 15 cm/6 inches long. Flatten the sides and top to square off the log to 5 cm/2 inches high. Wrap in clingfilm and chill in the refrigerator for 30–60 minutes. Add the cocoa powder to the other half of the dough and mix well. Shape into a flattened log the same size as the first one, wrap in clingfilm and chill in the refrigerator for 30–60 minutes.

Unwrap the dough and cut each flattened log lengthways into 3 slices. Cut each slice lengthways into 3 strips. Brush the strips with egg white and stack them in 3s, alternating the colours, so they are the same shape as the original logs. Wrap in clingfilm and chill in the refrigerator for 30–60 minutes.

Preheat the oven to 190°C/375°F/Gas Mark 5. Line 2 baking trays with baking paper.

Unwrap the logs and cut into slices with a sharp serrated knife. Put the cookies on the prepared baking trays, spaced well apart. Bake in the preheated oven for 12–15 minutes, until firm. Leave to cool for 5–10 minutes, then carefully transfer to wire racks to cool completely.

WALNUT & FIG PINWHEELS

Put the butter and 140 g/5 oz of the sugar into a bowl and mix well with a wooden spoon, then beat in the egg yolk. Sift the flour and salt into the mixture, add the ground walnuts and stir until thoroughly combined. Shape the dough into a ball, wrap in clingfilm and chill for 30–60 minutes.

Meanwhile, put the remaining sugar into a saucepan and stir in the water, then add the figs, mint tea and chopped mint. Bring to the boil, stirring constantly, until the sugar has dissolved, then lower the heat and simmer gently, stirring occasionally, for 5 minutes. Remove the pan from the heat and leave to cool.

Unwrap the dough and roll out between 2 sheets of baking paper into a 30-cm/12-inch square. Spread the fig filling evenly over the dough, then roll up like a Swiss roll. Wrap in clingfilm and chill in the refrigerator for 30 minutes.

Preheat the oven to 190°C/375°F/Gas Mark 5. Line 2 baking trays with baking paper.

Unwrap the roll and cut into thin slices with a sharp serrated knife. Put the slices on the prepared baking trays, spaced well apart. Bake in the preheated oven for 10–15 minutes, until golden brown. Leave to cool on the baking trays for 5–10 minutes, then transfer to wire racks to cool completely.

Makes about 30
225 g/8 oz butter, softened

200 g/7 oz caster sugar

1 egg yolk, lightly beaten

225 g/8 oz plain flour

pinch of salt

55 g/2 oz ground walnuts

125 ml/4 fl oz water

280 g/10 oz dried figs, finely chopped

5 tbsp freshly brewed mint tea

2 tsp finely chopped fresh mint

ICED CHERRY RINGS

Makes about 18

115 g/4 oz unsalted butter,
plus extra for greasing

85 g/3 oz golden caster sugar

1 egg yolk

finely grated rind of ½ lemon

200 g/7 oz plain flour, plus extra
for dusting

55 g/2 oz glacé cherries,
finely chopped

Icing

85 g/3 oz icing sugar

1½ tbsp lemon juice

Preheat the oven to 200°C/400°F/Gas Mark 6. Lightly
grease 2 baking trays.

Cream together the butter and caster sugar until pale
and fluffy. Beat in the egg yolk and lemon rind. Sift in the
flour, stir, then add the glacé cherries, mixing with your
hands to a soft dough.

Roll out the dough on a lightly floured surface to about
5 mm/¼ inch thick. Stamp out 8-cm/3¼ inch rounds
with a biscuit cutter. Stamp out the centre of each with
a 2.5-cm/1-inch round cutter and place the rings on
the prepared baking trays. Re-roll any trimmings and cut
more biscuits.

Bake in the preheated oven for 12–15 minutes, until firm
and golden brown.

Allow to cool on the baking trays for 2 minutes, then
transfer to a wire rack to cool completely.

Mix the icing sugar to a smooth paste with the lemon
juice. Drizzle over the biscuits and leave until set.

CAPPUCCINO COOKIES

Empty the cappuccino sachets into a small bowl and stir in the hot water to make a paste.

Put the butter and sugar into a bowl and mix well with a wooden spoon, then beat in the egg yolk and cappuccino paste. Sift together the flour and salt into the mixture and stir until thoroughly combined. Halve the dough, wrap in clingfilm and chill in the refrigerator for 30–60 minutes.

Preheat the oven to 190°C/375°F/Gas Mark 5. Line 2 baking trays with baking paper.

Unwrap the dough and roll out between 2 sheets of baking paper. Stamp out cookies with a 6-cm/2½-inch round cutter and put them on the prepared baking trays, spaced well apart.

Bake in the preheated oven for 10–12 minutes, until golden brown. Leave to cool for 5–10 minutes, then carefully transfer to wire racks to cool completely.

When the cookies are cool, place the wire racks over a sheet of baking paper. Put the chocolate into a heatproof bowl and set over a pan of gently simmering water until melted. Remove the bowl from the heat and leave to cool, then spoon the chocolate over the cookies. Gently tap the wire racks to level the surface and leave to set. Dust lightly with cocoa powder before serving.

Makes about 30

2 sachets instant cappuccino powder

1 tbsp hot water

225 g/8 oz butter, softened

140 g/5 oz caster sugar

1 egg yolk, lightly beaten

280 g/10 oz plain flour

pinch of salt

175 g/6 oz white chocolate, broken into pieces

cocoa powder, for dusting

CRANBERRY & COCONUT COOKIES

Makes about 30

225 g/8 oz butter, softened

140 g/5 oz caster sugar

1 egg yolk, lightly beaten

2 tsp vanilla extract

280 g/10 oz plain flour

pinch of salt

40 g/1½ oz desiccated coconut

60 g/2¼ oz dried cranberries

Preheat the oven to 190°C/375°F/Gas Mark 5. Line 2 baking trays with baking paper.

Put the butter and sugar into a bowl and mix well with a wooden spoon, then beat in the egg yolk and vanilla extract. Sift together the flour and salt into the mixture, add the coconut and cranberries and stir until thoroughly combined.

Scoop up tablespoons of the dough and place in mounds on the prepared baking trays, spaced well apart.

Bake in the preheated oven for 12–15 minutes, until golden brown. Leave to cool on the baking trays for 5–10 minutes, then carefully transfer to wire racks to cool completely.

CRUNCHY NUT & HONEY SANDWICH COOKIES

Preheat the oven to 190°C/375°F/Gas Mark 5. Line 2 baking trays with baking paper.

Put 225 g/8 oz of the butter and the caster sugar into a bowl and mix well with a wooden spoon, then beat in the egg yolk and vanilla extract. Sift together the flour and salt into the mixture and stir until thoroughly combined.

Scoop up tablespoons of the dough and roll into balls. Put half of them on 1 of the prepared baking trays, spaced well apart, and flatten gently. Spread out the nuts in a shallow dish and dip one side of the remaining dough balls into them, then place on the other baking tray, nut side uppermost, and flatten gently.

Bake in the preheated oven for 10–15 minutes, until light golden brown. Leave to cool on the baking trays for 5–10 minutes, then carefully transfer to wire racks to cool completely.

Beat the remaining butter with the icing sugar and honey until creamy and thoroughly mixed. Spread the honey mixture over the plain cookies and top with the nut-coated cookies.

Makes about 30

300 g/10½ oz butter, softened

140 g/5 oz caster sugar

1 egg yolk, lightly beaten

2 tsp vanilla extract

280 g/10 oz plain flour

pinch of salt

40 g/1½ oz macadamia nuts, cashew nuts or pine kernels, chopped

85 g/3 oz icing sugar

85 g/3 oz clover or other set honey

SNICKERDOODLES

Makes about 40

225 g/8 oz butter, softened
140 g/5 oz caster sugar
2 large eggs, lightly beaten
1 tsp vanilla extract
400 g/14 oz plain flour
1 tsp bicarbonate of soda
½ tsp freshly grated nutmeg
pinch of salt
55 g/2 oz pecan nuts, finely chopped

Cinnamon coating

1 tbsp caster sugar
2 tbsp ground cinnamon

Put the butter and sugar into a bowl and mix well with a wooden spoon, then beat in the eggs and vanilla extract. Sift together the flour, bicarbonate of soda, nutmeg and salt into the mixture, add the pecan nuts and stir until thoroughly combined. Shape the dough into a ball, wrap in clingfilm and chill in the refrigerator for 30–60 minutes.

Preheat the oven to 190°C/375°F/Gas Mark 5. Line 2 baking trays with baking paper.

For the cinnamon coating, mix together the caster sugar and cinnamon in a shallow dish. Scoop up tablespoons of the cookie dough and roll into balls. Roll each ball in the cinnamon mixture to coat and place on the prepared baking trays, spaced well apart.

Bake in the preheated oven for 10–12 minutes, until golden brown. Leave to cool on the baking trays for 5–10 minutes, then carefully transfer to wire racks to cool completely.

VIENNESE FINGERS

Preheat the oven to 160°C/325°F/Gas Mark 3. Lightly grease 2 baking trays.

Place the butter, sugar and vanilla extract in a bowl and cream together until pale and fluffy. Stir in the flour, mixing evenly to a fairly stiff dough.

Place the mixture in a piping bag fitted with a large star nozzle and pipe about 16 fingers, each 6 cm/2½ inches long, onto the prepared baking trays.

Bake in the preheated oven for 10–15 minutes, until pale golden. Cool for 2–3 minutes on the baking trays, then lift carefully onto a cooling rack with a palette knife to finish cooling.

Place the chocolate in a small heatproof bowl set over a pan of gently simmering water until melted. Remove from the heat. Dip the ends of each biscuit into the chocolate to coat, then place on a sheet of baking paper and leave to set.

Makes about 16

100 g/3½ oz unsalted butter, plus extra for greasing
25 g/1 oz golden caster sugar
½ tsp vanilla extract
100 g/3½ oz self-raising flour
100 g/3½ oz plain chocolate

ALMOND MACAROONS

Makes 12–14

1 egg white

85 g/3 oz ground almonds

85 g/3 oz caster sugar, plus extra for rolling

½ tsp almond extract

6–7 blanched almonds, split in half

Preheat the oven to 180°C/350°F/Gas Mark 4. Line 2 baking trays with baking paper.

Beat the egg white with a fork until frothy, then stir in the ground almonds, sugar and almond extract, mixing to form a sticky dough.

Using lightly sugared hands, roll the dough into small balls and place on the prepared baking trays. Press an almond half into the centre of each.

Bake in the preheated oven for 15–20 minutes, or until pale golden. Place on a wire rack to cool.

LEBKUCHEN

Preheat the oven to 180°C/350°F/Gas Mark 4. Line several baking trays with baking paper.

Put the eggs and sugar in a heatproof bowl set over a saucepan of gently simmering water. Whisk until thick and foamy. Remove the bowl from the saucepan and continue to whisk for 2 minutes.

Sift the flour, cocoa powder, cinnamon, cardamom, cloves and nutmeg into the bowl and stir in with the ground almonds and mixed peel. Drop heaped teaspoonfuls of the mixture onto the prepared baking trays, spreading them gently into smooth mounds.

Bake in the preheated oven for 15–20 minutes, until light brown and slightly soft to the touch. Cool on the baking trays for 10 minutes, then transfer to wire racks to cool completely.

Put the plain and white chocolate in 2 separate heatproof bowls set over 2 saucepans of gently simmering water until melted. Dip half the biscuits in the melted plain chocolate and half in the white chocolate. Sprinkle with sugar crystals and leave to set.

Makes 60

3 eggs
200 g/7 oz golden caster sugar
55 g/2 oz plain flour
2 tsp cocoa powder
1 tsp ground cinnamon
½ tsp ground cardamom
¼ tsp ground cloves
¼ tsp ground nutmeg
175 g/6 oz ground almonds
55 g/2 oz chopped mixed peel

To decorate
115 g/4 oz plain chocolate
115 g/4 oz white chocolate
sugar crystals

ALMOND BISCOTTI

Makes 20–24

250 g/9 oz plain flour, plus extra for dusting

1 tsp baking powder

pinch of salt

150 g/5½ oz golden caster sugar

2 eggs, beaten

finely grated rind of 1 orange

100 g/3½ oz whole blanched almonds, lightly toasted

Preheat the oven to 180°C/350°F/Gas Mark 4, then lightly dust a baking tray with flour.

Sift the flour, baking powder and salt into a bowl. Add the sugar, eggs and orange rind and mix to a dough. Knead in the almonds.

Roll the dough into a ball, cut in half and roll out each portion into a log about 4 cm/1½ inches in diameter. Place the logs on the prepared baking tray and then bake in the preheated oven for 10 minutes. Remove from the oven and leave to cool for 5 minutes

Using a serrated knife, cut the logs into 1 cm/½ inch thick diagonal slices. Arrange the slices on the baking tray and return to the oven for 15 minutes, or until slightly golden. Transfer to a wire rack to cool and go crisp.

GOOEY

Dreamy desserts to indulge

APPLE PIE

To make the pastry, sift the flour and salt into a mixing bowl. Add the butter and lard and rub in with your fingertips until the mixture resembles fine breadcrumbs. Add the water and gather the mixture together into a dough. Wrap the dough and chill in the refrigerator for 30 minutes.

Preheat the oven to 220°C/425°F/Gas Mark 7. Roll out almost two thirds of the pastry thinly and use to line a deep 23-cm/9-inch pie plate or pie tin.

Mix the apples with the sugar and spice and pack into the pastry case. Add the water if needed, particularly if the apples are not very juicy.

Roll out the remaining pastry to form a lid. Dampen the edges of the pie rim with water and position the lid, pressing the edges firmly together. Trim and crimp the edges.

Using the trimmings, cut out leaves or other shapes to decorate the top of the pie. Dampen and attach. Glaze the top of the pie with beaten egg or milk, make 1 or 2 slits in the top and place the pie on a baking tray.

Bake in the preheated oven for 20 minutes, then reduce the oven temperature to 180°C/350°F/Gas Mark 4 and bake for a further 30 minutes, or until the pastry is a light golden brown. Serve hot or cold, sprinkled with sugar.

Serves 6

Pastry
350 g/12 oz plain flour

pinch of salt

85 g/3 oz butter or margarine, cut into small pieces

85 g/3 oz lard or white vegetable fat, cut into small pieces

about 6 tbsp cold water

beaten egg or milk, for glazing

Filling
750 g–1 kg/1 lb 10 oz–2 lb 4 oz cooking apples, peeled, cored and sliced

125 g/4½ oz soft light brown sugar or caster sugar, plus extra for sprinkling

½–1 tsp ground cinnamon, mixed spice or ground ginger

1–2 tbsp water (optional)

LATTICED CHERRY PIE

Serves 8

Pastry

140 g/5 oz plain flour, plus extra for dusting

¼ tsp baking powder

½ tsp mixed spice

½ tsp salt

50 g/1¾ oz caster sugar

55 g/2 oz cold unsalted butter, diced, plus extra for greasing

1 egg, beaten, plus extra for glazing

Filling

900 g/2 lb stoned fresh cherries, or canned cherries, drained

150 g/5½ oz caster sugar

½ tsp almond extract

2 tsp cherry brandy

¼ tsp mixed spice

2 tbsp cornflour

2 tbsp water

25 g/1 oz butter

To make the pastry, sift the flour and baking powder into a large bowl. Stir in the mixed spice, salt and sugar. Rub in the butter with your fingertips until the mixture resembles fine breadcrumbs. Add the beaten egg and mix to a firm dough. Cut the dough in half and roll each half into a ball. Wrap in clingfilm and chill in the refrigerator for 30 minutes.

Preheat the oven to 220°C/425°F/Gas Mark 7. Grease a 23-cm/9 inch round tart tin. Roll out the pastry into 2 x 30 cm/12-inch rounds and use 1 to line the tart tin.

To make the filling, put half the cherries and the sugar into a large saucepan. Bring to a simmer over a low heat, stirring, for 5 minutes, or until the sugar has dissolved. Stir in the almond extract, brandy and mixed spice. In a separate bowl, mix the cornflour and water to form a paste. Remove the saucepan from the heat, stir in the cornflour paste, then return to the heat and stir constantly until the mixture boils and thickens. Leave to cool a little. Stir in the remaining cherries, pour into the pastry case, then dot with the butter.

Cut the remaining pastry round into long strips about 1 cm/½ inch wide. Lay 5 strips evenly across the top of the filling in the same direction. Now lay 6 strips crossways over the strips, folding under every other strip to form a lattice. Trim off the edges and seal with water. Use your fingers to crimp around the rim, then brush the top with beaten egg. Cover with foil, then bake in the preheated oven for 30 minutes. Discard the foil, then bake for a further 15 minutes, or until golden.

LEMON MERINGUE PIE

To make the pastry, sift the flour into a large bowl. Add the butter and rub it in with your fingertips until the mixture resembles fine breadcrumbs. Mix in the remaining ingredients. Knead briefly on a lightly floured work surface. Leave to rest for 30 minutes.

Preheat the oven to 180°C/350°F/Gas Mark 4. Grease a 20-cm/8-inch round tart tin.

Roll out the pastry to a thickness of 5 mm/¼ inch and use to line the prepared tin. Prick with a fork, then line with baking paper and fill with baking beans. Bake in the preheated oven for 15 minutes. Remove from the oven, then reduce the oven temperature to 150°C/300°F/Gas Mark 2.

To make the filling, mix the cornflour with a little water to form a paste. Pour the remaining water into a saucepan. Stir in the lemon juice and rind and the cornflour paste. Bring to the boil, stirring, and cook for 2 minutes. Cool slightly, then stir in 5 tablespoons of the sugar and the egg yolks and pour into the pastry case. Whisk the egg whites in a separate bowl until stiff. Gradually whisk in the remaining sugar and spread over the pie.

Bake in the oven for 40 minutes, or until the meringue is light brown. Serve with cream.

Serves 6

Pastry

200 g/7 oz plain flour, plus extra for dusting

100 g/3½ oz butter, diced, plus extra for greasing

50 g/1¾ oz icing sugar, sifted

finely grated rind of 1 lemon

1 egg yolk, beaten

3 tbsp milk

Filling

3 tbsp cornflour

300 ml/10 fl oz cold water

juice and grated rind of 2 lemons

175 g/6 oz caster sugar

2 eggs, separated

single cream, to serve

STRAWBERRY CHEESECAKE

Serves 8

Base

55 g/2 oz unsalted butter

200 g/7 oz digestive biscuits, crushed

85 g/3 oz chopped walnuts

Filling

450 g/1 lb mascarpone cheese

2 eggs, beaten

3 tbsp caster sugar

250 g/9 oz white chocolate, broken into pieces

300 g/10½ oz strawberries, hulled and quartered

Topping

175 g/6 oz mascarpone cheese

50 g/1¾ oz white chocolate shavings

4 strawberries, halved

Preheat the oven to 150°C/300°F/Gas Mark 2.

Melt the butter in a saucepan over a low heat and stir in the crushed biscuits and walnuts. Spoon into a 23-cm/9-inch round springform cake tin and press evenly over the base with the back of a spoon. Set aside.

To make the filling, beat the mascarpone cheese in a bowl until smooth, then beat in the eggs and sugar. Melt the white chocolate in a heatproof bowl set over a saucepan of gently simmering water, stirring until smooth. Remove from the heat and leave to cool slightly, then stir into the cheese mixture. Stir in the strawberries.

Spoon the mixture into the cake tin, spread out evenly and smooth the surface. Bake in the preheated oven for 1 hour, or until the filling is just firm. Turn off the oven and leave the cheesecake to cool inside with the door slightly ajar until completely cold. Transfer to a serving plate.

For the topping, spread the mascarpone cheese on top. Decorate with the chocolate shavings and the strawberry halves.

WHITE TRUFFLE CAKE

Preheat the oven to 180°C/ 350°F/Gas Mark 4. Grease and line the base of a 20-cm/8-inch round springform cake tin.

Melt the chocolate in a heatproof bowl set over a saucepan of gently simmering water.

Using a electric hand-held whisk, beat the eggs and sugar together in a large bowl until thick and pale – the mixture should leave a trail when the whisk is lifted. Sift the flour and gently fold into the egg mixture with a metal spoon or palette knife. Add the melted chocolate.

Pour the mixture into the prepared tin and bake in the preheated oven for 25 minutes, or until springy to the touch. Leave to cool slightly in the tin, then transfer to a wire rack and leave to cool completely. Return the cold cake to the tin.

To make the topping, put the cream in a saucepan and bring to the boil, stirring constantly. Leave to cool slightly, then add the chocolate and stir until melted and combined. Remove from the heat and set aside until almost cool, stirring, then mix in the mascarpone cheese.

Pour on top of the cake. Chill in the refrigerator for 2 hours. Decorate with the chocolate shavings before serving.

Serves 12

butter, for greasing
50 g/1¾ oz white chocolate
2 eggs
50 g/1¾ oz caster sugar
70 g/2½ oz plain flour

Truffle topping

300 ml/10 fl oz double cream
350 g/12 oz white chocolate, broken into pieces
250 g/9 oz mascarpone cheese
50 g/1¾ oz white chocolate shavings

TREACLE TART

Roll out the pastry on a lightly floured work surface and use to line a 20-cm/8-inch round loose-based tart tin, reserving the pastry trimmings. Prick the base of the pastry case all over with a fork, cover with clingfilm and chill in the refrigerator for 30 minutes. Re-roll the reserved pastry trimmings and cut out small shapes, such as leaves, stars or hearts, to decorate the top of the tart.

Preheat the oven to 190°C/375°F/Gas Mark 5.

Mix the golden syrup, breadcrumbs, double cream and lemon rind with the lemon juice in a small bowl. Pour the mixture into the pastry case and decorate the top of the tart with the pastry shapes.

Transfer to the preheated oven and bake for 35–40 minutes, or until the filling is just set.

Leave the tart to cool slightly in the tin before turning out and serving with cream.

Serves 8

250 g/ 9 oz ready-made shortcrust pastry

plain flour, for dusting

350 g/12 oz golden syrup

125 g/4½ oz fresh white breadcrumbs

125 ml/4 fl oz double cream

finely grated rind of ½ lemon or orange

2 tbsp lemon juice or orange juice

whipped cream or clotted cream, to serve

BANOFFEE PIE

Place the unopened cans of milk in a large saucepan and add enough water to cover them completely. Bring to the boil, then reduce the heat and simmer for 2 hours, topping up the water level to keep the cans covered. Carefully lift out the hot cans and leave to cool.

Preheat the oven to 180°C/350°F/Gas Mark 4. Grease a 23-cm/9-inch round tart tin.

For the biscuit base, put the butter in a bowl and add the crushed biscuits and ground nuts. Mix together well, then press the mixture evenly over the base and sides of the tart tin. Bake in the preheated oven for 10–12 minutes, then remove from the oven and leave to cool.

Peel and slice the bananas and put in a bowl. Add the lemon juice and vanilla extract and mix together. Spread the banana mixture over the biscuit base, then spoon the contents of the cooled cans of condensed milk over the bananas. Sprinkle over 50 g/1¾ oz of the chocolate, then top with a layer of whipped cream. Sprinkle over the remaining grated chocolate and serve the pie at room temperature.

Serves 4–6

Filling

2 x 400-g/14-oz cans condensed milk

4 ripe bananas

juice of ½ lemon

1 tsp vanilla extract

75 g/2¾ oz plain chocolate, grated

450 ml/16 fl oz double cream, whipped

Biscuit base

85 g/3 oz butter, melted, plus extra for greasing

150 g/5½ oz digestive biscuits, crushed

50 g/1¾ oz shelled almonds, toasted and ground

50 g/1¾ oz shelled hazelnuts, toasted and ground

PECAN PIE

Serves 8

Pastry
200 g/7 oz plain flour, plus extra for dusting

115 g/4 oz unsalted butter

2 tbsp caster sugar

Filling
70 g/2½ oz unsalted butter

100 g/3½ oz light muscovado sugar

140 g/5 oz golden syrup

2 large eggs, beaten

1 tsp vanilla extract

115 g/4 oz pecan nuts

For the pastry, place the flour in a bowl and rub in the butter with your fingertips until it resembles fine breadcrumbs. Stir in the caster sugar and add enough cold water to mix to a firm dough. Wrap in clingfilm and chill for 15 minutes, or until firm enough to roll out.

Preheat the oven to 200°C/400°F/Gas Mark 6. Roll out the pastry on a lightly floured surface and use to line a 23-cm/9-inch round loose-based tart tin. Prick the base with a fork. Chill for 15 minutes.

Place the tart tin on a baking tray and line with a sheet of baking paper and baking beans. Bake blind in the preheated oven for 10 minutes. Remove the baking beans and paper and bake for a further 5 minutes. Reduce the oven temperature to 180°C/350°F/Gas Mark 4.

For the filling, place the butter, muscovado sugar and golden syrup in a saucepan and heat gently until melted. Remove from the heat and quickly beat in the eggs and vanilla extract.

Roughly chop the pecan nuts and stir into the mixture. Pour into the pastry case and bake for 35–40 minutes, until the filling is just set. Serve warm or cold.

SWEET PUMPKIN PIE

Preheat the oven to 190°C/375°F/Gas Mark 5. Put the pumpkin halves, face down, in a baking tin and cover with foil. Bake in the preheated oven for 1½ hours. Scoop out the flesh and purée in a food processor. Drain off any excess liquid.

Grease a 23-cm/9-inch round tart tin. Sift the flour and baking powder into a bowl. Stir in ½ teaspoon of the cinnamon, ¼ teaspoon of the nutmeg, ¼ teaspoon of the cloves, ½ teaspoon of the salt and the caster sugar. Rub in the butter with your fingertips until the mixture resembles breadcrumbs. Lightly beat one of the eggs, then add to the bowl. Mix together to form a dough, then shape into a ball. Roll out on a lightly floured surface and use to line the prepared tin. Chill for 30 minutes.

Preheat the oven to 220°C/425°F/Gas Mark 7. Put the pumpkin in a bowl, then stir in the condensed milk and the remaining eggs. Add the remaining spices and salt, then stir in the vanilla extract and demerara sugar. Pour into the pastry case and bake in the preheated oven for 15 minutes.

Meanwhile, make the topping. Mix the flour, demerara sugar and cinnamon in a bowl, rub in the butter, then stir in the nuts. Remove the pie from the oven and reduce the heat to 180°C/350°F/Gas Mark 4. Sprinkle over the topping, then bake for a further 35 minutes.

Serves 6

1.8 kg/4 lb sweet pumpkin, halved and deseeded

140 g/5 oz plain flour, plus extra for dusting

¼ tsp baking powder

1½ tsp ground cinnamon

¾ tsp ground nutmeg

¾ tsp ground cloves

1 tsp salt

50 g/1¾ oz caster sugar

55 g/2 oz cold unsalted butter, diced, plus extra for greasing

3 eggs

400 g/14 oz canned condensed milk

½ tsp vanilla extract

1 tbsp demerara sugar

Streusel topping

2 tbsp plain flour

4 tbsp demerara sugar

1 tsp ground cinnamon

2 tbsp cold unsalted butter, diced

75 g/2¾ oz pecan nuts, chopped

75 g/2¾ oz walnuts, chopped

SWEET POTATO PIE

Serves 8

Pastry

175 g/6 oz plain flour, plus extra for dusting

½ tsp salt

¼ tsp caster sugar

50 g/1¾ oz butter, diced

40 g/1½ oz white vegetable fat, diced

2–2½ tbsp cold water

filling

500 g/1 lb 2 oz orange-fleshed sweet potatoes, peeled

3 eggs, beaten

100 g/3½ oz soft light brown sugar

350 g/12 oz canned condensed milk

40 g/1½ oz butter, melted

2 tsp vanilla extract

1 tsp ground cinnamon

1 tsp ground nutmeg

½ tsp salt

To make the pastry, sift the flour, salt and caster sugar into a bowl. Add the butter and white vegetable fat to the bowl and rub in with your fingertips until the mixture resembles fine breadcrumbs. Sprinkle over 2 tablespoons of the water and mix with a fork to make a soft dough. If the pastry is too dry, sprinkle over the remaining water. Wrap in clingfilm and chill in the refrigerator for at least 1 hour.

Meanwhile, bring a large saucepan of water to the boil over a high heat. Add the sweet potatoes and cook for 15 minutes. Drain, then cool under cold running water. When cool, cut each into eight wedges. Place the potatoes in a bowl and beat in the eggs and brown sugar until very smooth. Beat in the remaining ingredients, then set aside.

Preheat the oven to 220°C/425°F/Gas Mark 7. Roll out the pastry on a lightly floured work surface into a thin 28-cm/11-inch round and use to line a 23 cm/9-inch round tart tin, about 4 cm/1½ inches deep. Trim off the excess pastry and press a floured fork around the edge. Prick the base of the pastry case all over with the fork. Line with baking paper and fill with baking beans. Bake in the preheated oven for 12 minutes, until lightly golden. Remove from the oven and take out the paper and beans.

Pour the filling into the pastry case and return to the oven for a further 10 minutes. Reduce the oven temperature to 160°C/325°F/Gas Mark 3 and bake for a further 35 minutes, or until a knife inserted into the centre comes out clean. Leave to cool on a wire rack. Serve warm or at room temperature.

STRAWBERRY TARTLETS

To make the pastry, sift the flour and icing sugar into a bowl. Add the butter to the flour mixture with the egg yolk, mixing with your fingertips and adding a little water, if necessary, to mix to a soft dough. Cover and chill in the refrigerator for 15 minutes.

Preheat the oven to 200°C/400°F/Gas Mark 6. Roll out the pastry and use to line 4 x 9-cm/ 3½-inch tartlet tins. Prick the bases with a fork, line with baking paper and fill with baking beans, then bake blind in the preheated oven for 10 minutes. Remove the paper and beans and bake for a further 5 minutes, until golden brown. Remove from the oven and cool.

For the filling, place the vanilla pod in a saucepan with the milk and leave on a low heat to infuse, without boiling, for 10 minutes. Whisk the egg yolks, caster sugar, flour and cornflour together in a mixing bowl until smooth. Strain the milk into the bowl and whisk until smooth. Pour the mixture back into the pan and stir over a medium heat until boiling. Cook, stirring constantly, for about 2 minutes, until thickened and smooth. Remove from the heat and fold in the whipped cream. Spoon the mixture into the pastry cases.

When the filling has set slightly, top with strawberries, then spoon over a little redcurrant jelly to glaze.

Serves 8

Pastry

125 g/4½ oz plain flour

2 tbsp icing sugar

70 g/2½ oz unsalted butter, cut into pieces, softened

1 egg yolk

1–2 tbsp water

Filling

1 vanilla pod, split

200 ml/7 fl oz milk

2 egg yolks

40 g/1½ oz caster sugar

1 tbsp plain flour

1 tbsp cornflour

125 ml/4 fl oz double cream, softly whipped

350 g/12 oz strawberries, hulled and halved

4 tbsp redcurrant jelly, melted

BAKLAVA

Makes 25

225 g/8 oz walnut halves

225 g/8 oz shelled pistachio nuts

100 g/3½ oz blanched almonds

4 tbsp pine kernels, finely chopped

finely grated rind of 2 large oranges

6 tbsp sesame seeds

1 tbsp sugar

½ tsp ground cinnamon

½ tsp mixed spice

23 sheets filo pastry, thawed if frozen

250 g/9 oz butter, melted, plus extra for greasing

Syrup

450 g/1 lb castor sugar

450 ml/16 fl oz water

5 tbsp honey

3 cloves

2 large strips of lemon zest

To make the filling, put the walnuts, pistachio nuts, almonds and pine kernels in a food processor and process gently, until finely chopped but not ground. Transfer the chopped nuts to a bowl and stir in the orange rind, sesame seeds, sugar, cinnamon and mixed spice.

Grease a 25-cm/10-inch square ovenproof dish, about 5 cm/2 inches deep. Preheat the oven to 160°C/325°F/ Gas Mark 3. Cut the stacked filo sheets to size, using a ruler. Keep the sheets covered with a damp cloth. Place a sheet of filo on the bottom of the dish and brush with melted butter. Top with 7 more sheets, brushing with butter between each layer.

Sprinkle with a generous 150 g/5 oz of the nutty filling. Top with 3 sheets of filo, brushing each one with butter. Continue layering until you have used up all the filo and filling, ending with a top layer of 3 filo sheets. Brush with butter.

Using a sharp knife cut the baklava into 5-cm/2-inch squares. Brush again with butter. Bake in the preheated oven for 1 hour.

Meanwhile, put all the syrup ingredients in a saucepan. Slowly bring to the boil, stirring to dissolve the sugar, then simmer for 15 minutes, without stirring, until a thin syrup forms. Leave to cool.

Remove the baklava from the oven and strain the syrup over the top. Leave to cool in the dish, then cut out the squares to serve.

STICKY TOFFEE PUDDING

Preheat the oven to 180°C/350°F/Gas Mark 4. Grease a 20-cm/8-inch round cake tin.

To make the pudding, put the sultanas, dates and bicarbonate of soda into a heatproof bowl. Cover with boiling water and leave to soak. Put the butter into a separate bowl, add the sugar and mix well. Beat in the eggs, then fold in the flour. Drain the soaked fruit, add to the bowl and mix.

Spoon the mixture evenly into the prepared cake tin. Bake in the preheated oven for 35–40 minutes, or until a skewer inserted into the centre comes out clean.

About 5 minutes before the end of the cooking time, make the sauce. Melt the butter in a saucepan over a medium heat. Stir in the cream and sugar and bring to the boil, stirring constantly. Reduce the heat and simmer for 5 minutes.

Turn out the pudding onto a serving plate and pour over the sauce.

Serves 6–8

Pudding
75 g/2¾ oz sultanas

150 g/5½ oz stoned dates, chopped

1 tsp bicarbonate of soda

25 g/1 oz butter, plus extra for greasing

200 g/7 oz soft light brown sugar

2 eggs

200 g/7 oz self-raising flour, sifted

Sticky toffee sauce
25 g/1 oz butter

175 ml/6 fl oz double cream

200 g/7 oz soft light brown sugar

PEAR & TOFFEE CRUMBLE

Serves 4

Crumble topping
115 g/4 oz self raising flour

100 g/3½ oz unsalted butter, diced

5 tbsp demerara sugar

2 tbsp finely chopped hazelnuts

Filling
3 tbsp golden syrup

3 tbsp demerara sugar

25 g/1 oz unsalted butter

2 tbsp single cream

½ tsp vanilla extract

4 large pears

vanilla ice cream, to serve

Preheat the oven to 200°C/400°F/Gas Mark 6.

To make the crumble topping, put the flour in a large heatproof bowl, then rub in the butter with your fingertips until the mixture resembles fine breadcrumbs. Stir in 4 tablespoons of the sugar and the chopped hazelnuts, then cook in the preheated oven for 5–10 minutes, until heated through.

To make the toffee, put the golden syrup into a saucepan over a low heat. Add the sugar, half the butter, the cream and vanilla extract, and bring gently to the boil. Simmer for 3 minutes, stirring constantly, then remove from the heat and set aside.

Put the remaining butter in a frying pan and melt over a low heat. Meanwhile, peel and roughly chop the pears, then add them to the pan and cook, stirring gently, for 3 minutes. Stir in the toffee and continue to cook, stirring, over a low heat for another 3 minutes.

Transfer the pear mixture to an ovenproof baking dish. Arrange the crumble evenly over the top, then sprinkle over the remaining sugar. Bake in the preheated oven for 25–30 minutes, or until the crumble is golden brown.

Serve hot with vanilla ice cream.

BAKED APPLES

Preheat the oven to 180°C/350°F/Gas Mark 4.

Place the honey and ginger syrup in a saucepan and heat until the honey has melted. Stir in the oats and cook gently over a low heat for 2 minutes. Remove the saucepan from the heat and stir in the almonds, apricots and stem ginger.

Core the apples, widen the tops slightly and score around the circumference of each to prevent the skins from bursting during cooking. Place them in an ovenproof dish and fill the cavities with the stuffing.

Pour just enough water into the dish to come about one third of the way up the apples. Bake in the preheated oven for 40 minutes, or until tender. Serve immediately.

Makes 4

1 tbsp clear honey

1 piece stem ginger, drained and finely chopped, plus 1 tbsp syrup from the jar

4 tbsp rolled oats

25 g/1 oz blanched almonds, finely chopped

55 g/2 oz dried apricots, finely chopped

4 large cooking apples

CRÊPES SUZETTE

Makes 8

Crêpes

115 g/4 oz plain flour

pinch of salt

2 tbsp caster sugar

2 large eggs

300 ml/10 fl oz milk

30 g/1 oz butter, melted and cooled

finely grated rind of 1 lemon

sunflower oil, for brushing

Orange sauce

55 g/2 oz caster sugar

1 tbsp water

finely grated rind of 1 large orange

125 ml/4 fl oz orange juice

55 g/2 oz unsalted butter, diced

1 tbsp orange liqueur

2 tbsp brandy

To make the crêpes, sift the flour, salt and sugar into a large bowl and make a well in the centre. Put the eggs and a little of the milk into the well and beat them together, gradually drawing in the flour. Stir in the butter, then slowly add the remaining milk until the batter has the consistency of single cream. Stir in the lemon rind. Cover and leave to stand for at least 30 minutes.

Heat a 20-cm/8-inch frying pan over a high heat, then lightly brush with oil. Reduce the heat to medium, add a ladleful of batter to the pan and swirl around so it covers the base thinly. Cook for 1 minute, or until the underside is cooked and golden. Use a spatula to flip over the crêpe and cook on the other side. Transfer to a plate. Cook the remaining batter, stacking the crêpes on the plate with baking paper between each one.

To make the orange sauce, place the sugar in a large frying pan over a medium heat and stir in the water. Continue stirring until the sugar dissolves, then increase the heat to high and bubble for 1–2 minutes, until it just begins to turn golden brown. Stir in the orange rind and juice, then add the butter and stir until it melts. Add the liqueur.

Lay one of the crêpes flat in the pan and spoon over the sauce. Fold the crêpe into quarters and push to one side of the pan. Add the next crêpe, spoon over the sauce and fold as before. Repeat until all the crêpes are coated with the sauce and folded. Remove the pan from the heat. Warm the brandy in a small saucepan, ignite and carefully pour it over the crêpes to flambé, shaking the frying pan. When the flames die down, serve the crêpes with the sauce spooned over.

CRÈME BRÛLÉE

Prepare the fruit, if necessary, and lightly rinse, then place in the bases of 4–6 x 150-ml/5-fl oz ramekin dishes. Sprinkle the fruit with the liqueur.

Cream the mascarpone cheese in a bowl until soft, then gradually beat in the crème fraîche.

Spoon the cheese mixture over the fruit, smoothing the surface and ensuring that the tops are level. Chill in the refrigerator for at least 2 hours.

Sprinkle the tops with the sugar. Using a chef's blow torch, grill the tops until caramelized (about 2–3 minutes). Alternatively, cook under a preheated grill, turning the dishes, for 3–4 minutes, or until the tops are lightly caramelized all over.

Serve immediately or chill in the refrigerator for 15–20 minutes before serving.

Serves 4–6

225–300 g/8–10½ oz mixed soft fruits, such as blueberries and stoned fresh cherries

1½–2 tbsp orange liqueur or orange flower water

250 g/9 oz mascarpone cheese

200 ml/7 fl oz crème fraîche

2–3 tbsp dark muscovado sugar

PAVLOVA

Serves 6

4 egg whites
225 g/8 oz caster sugar
1 tsp cornflour
1 tsp white wine vinegar
1 tsp vanilla extract
300 ml/10 fl oz double cream
1 tbsp caster sugar
2 tbsp framboise liqueur
175 g/6 oz fresh raspberries
55 g/2 oz plain chocolate shavings

Preheat the oven to 150°C/300°F/Gas 2.

In a large mixing bowl, whisk the egg whites until stiff and gradually whisk in 115 g/4 oz of the sugar. In a separate bowl, mix the remaining sugar with the cornflour and then whisk it into the egg white mixture; it should be very shiny and firm. Quickly fold the vinegar and vanilla extract into the egg white mixture.

Draw a 25 cm/10-inch circle on a sheet of baking paper, turn the paper over and place it on a baking tray. Pile the egg white mixture onto the baking paper and spread evenly to the edge of the circle; swirl it around on top to make an attractive shape. Bake in the centre of the preheated oven for 1 hour.

Remove from the oven and leave to cool slightly, then peel off the paper. Place the meringue on a large serving plate. It will shrink and crack but do not worry about this.

An hour before serving, whip together the cream, sugar and liquour until thick and floppy. Pile on top of the meringue and decorate with raspberries and chocolate shavings. Chill before serving.

TRIFLE

To make the fruit layer, spread the sponge cakes with jam, cut into bite-sized pieces and arrange in the bases of 4 individual serving dishes. Scatter over the fruit, pour over the sherry and set aside.

To make the custard, place the cream and vanilla extract in a saucepan and bring almost to the boil over a low heat. Meanwhile, place the egg yolks and sugar in a heatproof bowl and whisk together. Remove the cream mixture from the heat and gradually stir into the egg mixture. Return the mixture to the saucepan and warm over a low heat, stirring, until thickened. Remove the custard from the heat and leave to cool for 30 minutes, then pour it over the fruit layer. Cover with clingfilm and chill for 2½ hours.

Remove the dishes from the refrigerator. To make the topping, whip the cream and sugar together, then spread it evenly over the custard layer. Cover again with clingfilm and chill for a further 1½ hours. Sprinkle over the pistachio nuts and decorate with strawberries before serving.

Serves 4

Fruit layer

6 trifle sponge cakes

2 tbsp strawberry jam

6 large strawberries, hulled and sliced, plus extra to decorate

2 bananas, peeled and sliced

400 g/14 oz canned sliced peaches, drained

6 tbsp sherry

Custard layer

250 ml/9 fl oz double cream

1 tsp vanilla extract

3 egg yolks

4 tbsp caster sugar

Topping

300 ml/10 fl oz double cream

2 tbsp caster sugar

chopped pistachio nuts, to decorate

TIRAMISÙ

Serves 4

200 ml/7 fl oz strong black coffee, cooled to room temperature

4 tbsp orange liqueur

3 tbsp orange juice

16 Italian sponge fingers

250 g/9 oz mascarpone cheese

300 ml/10 fl oz double cream, lightly whipped

3 tbsp icing sugar

grated rind of 1 orange

To decorate

chopped toasted almonds

strips of lemon zest

chocolate shavings

Pour the cooled coffee into a jug and stir in the liqueur and orange juice. Put 2 of the sponge fingers in the base of each of 4 individual serving dishes, then pour over half of the coffee mixture.

Place the mascarpone cheese in a bowl with the cream, icing sugar and orange rind and mix together well. Spread half of the mascarpone mixture over the coffee-soaked sponge fingers, then arrange the remaining sponge fingers on top. Pour over the remaining coffee mixture and then spread over the remaining mascarpone mixture. Chill in the refrigerator for at least 2 hours

Serve decorated with chopped toasted almonds, strips of lemon zest and chocolate shavings.

BANANA & BROWN SUGAR RIPPLE DESSERTS

Preheat the oven to 190°C/375°F/Gas Mark 5.

Toss the pecan nuts in the caster sugar, scatter over a baking tray and roast in the preheated oven for 4–5 minutes, until golden. Remove from the oven and leave to cool, then roughly chop.

Spoon the yogurt into a large bowl and sprinkle the muscovado sugar evenly over the top. Leave for 5 minutes, or until the sugar begins to melt, and then fold it very lightly into the yogurt to create a rippled effect.

Peel and slice the bananas, then divide between 4 individual serving dishes. Carefully spoon over the yogurt, taking care to retain the rippled effect. Top with a scattering of the roasted pecan nuts and serve immediately.

Serves 4

50 g/1¾ oz pecan nuts
1 tsp caster sugar
750 g/1 lb 10 oz Greek-style yogurt
3 tbsp dark muscovado sugar
3 bananas

SYLLABUB

Serves 4–6

grated rind and juice of
1 lemon

125 ml/4 fl oz sweet white wine

2 tbsp brandy

55 g/2 oz caster sugar

300 ml/10 fl oz double cream

strips of lemon zest, to decorate

sponge fingers or ratafia
biscuits, to serve

Place the lemon rind and juice in a bowl together with
the wine and brandy. Cover and leave to infuse for a few
hours or overnight. Stir in the sugar until it has dissolved.

Whip the cream in a large bowl using an electric mixer.
When it starts to thicken, carefully pour in the liquid, a little
at a time, until it is all mixed in. The mixture should be very
thick and soft; do not over-whip it. Spoon into individual
serving glasses and chill for a few hours.

Decorate with strips of lemon zest and serve with sponge
fingers or ratafia biscuits.

MANGO SORBET

Using a sharp knife, thinly peel the mangoes, holding them over a bowl to catch the juices. Cut the flesh away from the central stone and put in a food processor or blender. Add the reserved mango juices, the lemon juice and salt and process to form a smooth purée. Push the mango purée through a nylon sieve into the bowl.

Put the sugar and water in a heavy-based saucepan and heat gently, stirring, until the sugar has dissolved. Bring to the boil, without stirring, then remove from the heat and leave to cool slightly.

Pour the syrup into the mango purée and mix well. Leave to cool, then chill the mango syrup in the refrigerator for 2 hours, or until cold.

If using an ice-cream machine, churn the mixture in the machine following the manufacturer's instructions. Alternatively, freeze the mixture in a freezerproof container, uncovered, for 3–4 hours, or until mushy. Tip the mixture into a bowl and stir with a fork or beat in a food processor to break down the ice crystals. Return to the freezer and freeze for a further 3–4 hours, or until firm. Cover the container with a lid for storing.

To serve, scoop into individual serving dishes and decorate with mango slices.

Serves 4–6

2 large ripe mangoes, plus extra slices to decorate

juice of 1 lemon

pinch of salt

115 g/4 oz caster sugar

3 tbsp water

BISCUIT TORTONI

Serves 6

125 g/4 oz amaretti biscuits
300 ml/10 fl oz double cream
150 ml/5 fl oz single cream
115 g/4 oz icing sugar
4 tbsp Marsala

Line a 450-g/1-lb loaf tin or 850-ml/1½-pint oblong freezerproof plastic container with clingfilm, allowing it to hang over the edges of the container so that the ice cream can be easily removed.

Put the biscuits in a food processor and process to form fine crumbs. Alternatively, put the biscuits in a strong polythene bag and crush with a rolling pin.

Pour the double cream and single cream into a large bowl and whip together until the mixture holds its shape. Sift the icing sugar into the whipped cream, then fold in with the Marsala. Fold in the biscuits, reserving a third.

Pour the mixture into the prepared tin, smooth the surface and freeze, uncovered, for 5 hours, or until firm. Cover the container with a lid for storing.

Take the ice cream out of the freezer about 30 minutes before you are ready to serve it. Uncover, turn out onto a serving dish and remove the clingfilm. Leave at room temperature to soften slightly. Using a palette knife, press the reserved crushed biscuits lightly onto the top and sides of the ice cream until it is evenly coated. Serve cut into thick slices.

HONEYCOMB ICE CREAM

Grease a baking tray. To make honeycomb, put the sugar and golden syrup in a heavy-based saucepan and heat gently until the sugar melts, then boil for 1–2 minutes, or until beginning to caramelize, being careful not to allow the mixture to burn. Stir in the bicarbonate of soda, then immediately pour the mixture onto the prepared baking tray but do not spread. Leave for about 10 minutes, until cold. When the honeycomb is cold, put it in a strong polythene bag and crush into small pieces, using a rolling pin or meat mallet.

Whip the cream until it holds its shape, then whisk in the condensed milk. If using an ice-cream machine, churn the mixture in the machine following the manufacturer's instructions. Just before the ice cream freezes, add the crushed honeycomb, reserving a little for decoration. Alternatively, freeze the mixture in a freezerproof container, uncovered, for 1–2 hours, or until it begins to set around the edges. Tip the mixture into a bowl and stir with a fork or beat in a food processor until smooth. Fold in the honeycomb pieces. Return to the freezer and freeze for a further 2–3 hours, or until firm. Cover the container with a lid for storing.

To serve, scoop into individual serving dishes and decorate with the reserved crushed honeycomb.

Serves 6–8
butter, for greasing
85 g/3 oz granulated sugar
2 tbsp golden syrup
1 tsp bicarbonate of soda
400 ml/14 fl oz whipping cream
400 g/14 oz canned condensed milk

Index